I0892921

CANAL FISHING

A Practical Guide

Dominic Garnett

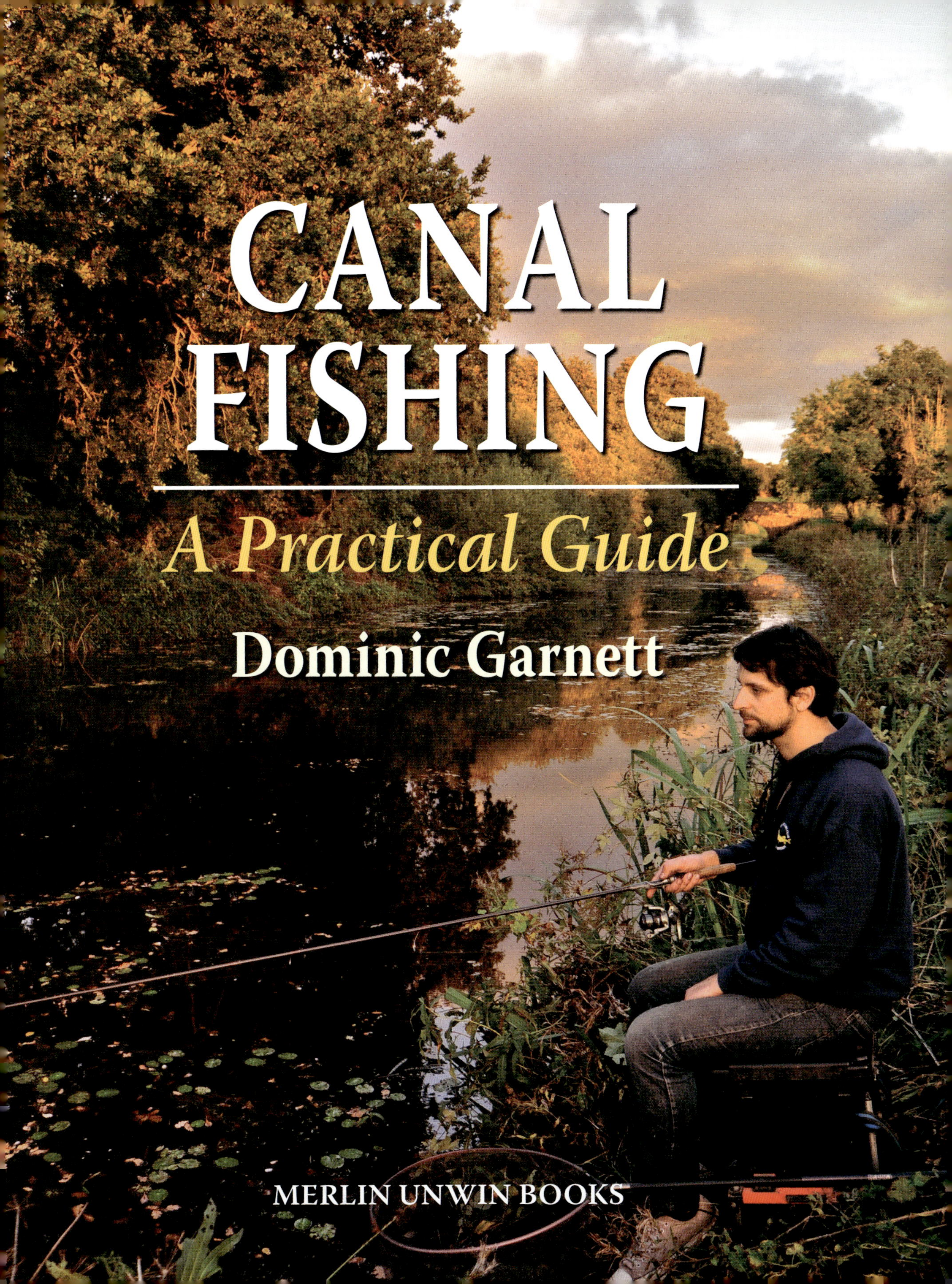

MERLIN UNWIN BOOKS

First published by Merlin Unwin Books, 2014
Text and illustrations © Dominic Garnett 2014

All rights reserved. No portion of this book may be reproduced, stored in a retrieval system or transmitted at any time or by any means mechanical, electronic, photocopying, recording or otherwise, without the prior, written permission of the publisher. All enquiries should be addressed to the publisher:

Merlin Unwin Books Limited
Palmers' House, 7 Corve Street,
Ludlow, Shropshire, SY8 1DB
www.merlinunwin.co.uk

The right of Dominic Garnett to be identified as the author of this work has been asserted by him in accordance with the Copyright, Designs and Patents Act 1988.

A CIP record of this book is available from the British Library.
Printed and bound by Latitude Press

ISBN 978-1-906122-64-5

CONTENTS

FOREWORD
by Des Taylor

The local canal was the very first place I cast a line. We started with cane poles, literally the sort of cane you'd find in the back garden. These were our first rods, set up with a piece of nylon tied to the end and a grayling float or a tiny piece of quill.

There was a chap who lived opposite us called Stan Poole, and he and his son Keith would take me fishing. Stan was a good angler. He'd catch twenty or so small fish every time we went, while I was lucky if I caught one! But that's where it all began for me and at that time I suppose it was about fishing rather than catching.

The canals represented lovely little parklands amongst all the industry. They also held lots of creatures for us to explore. We used to find great crested and palmate newts, and there was a lot of bird life. We built rafts and dipped nets, and I suppose that's where my interest in wildlife, bird-watching and fishing all first appeared.

Des Taylor with a beautiful canal perch from the Black Country.

The stretch of our canal had been a busy industrial area and there was still a coal yard being used, but it was very rich with fish. It hadn't got carp back then, but it had a lot of perch and roach. We struggled at first. Our hooks were too big. To catch a fish, any fish, was an incredible experience! My first-ever catch was a stone loach. Perch came next. The fish weren't big but we learned a lot about watercraft. There were little basins where the boats would come in that were great for fishing. There were also gas works where there was warm water that would draw the fish in.

The sad bit was that after I got married and left the area, the canal was badly polluted. We used to joke that even rats wouldn't live there. It was a terrible environment, full of rubbish.

Today, canals are on the way back. The work on them has been fantastic and they're probably more beautiful now than they've ever been. Some of the country canals have incredible views and are almost like rivers. But there's also real urban beauty when you fish by lock gates or the ironwork of old factories. A lot of the old engineering works and structures have hardly changed at all – back then things were built to last.

Eventually I went back and visited the canal where I first cast a line. It was better than ever! The estate was cleaned up; the bridge was still in good nick; there were reedmace, moorhens, coots and all sorts of insect life. The water was so rich! I went back to that very first spot I ever fished and there I caught perch, roach and lost a good tench.

The canals are now in the best condition they've been all my lifetime. They hold a heck of a lot of fish and plenty of big ones too. You wouldn't believe some of the fish that are in there and the true canal specialists make some terrific catches. In my area alone you've got specimen pike and zander. I've had big roach, specimen perch and eels to four pounds. You've got big canal carp – my mates have had them to over thirty pounds – and it's strange to think that there's probably more five-pound chub in the heart of the Black Country than in the River Thames these days.

We're talking about top, top class fishing. Be in no doubt, when you take a walk or cycle on a canal and you're half a mile from a bridge, you're probably trying spots that never get fished. Canals are now very much part of the modern fishing scene. Just about all methods work. You can leger boilies or pole fish, you can try spinning, drop shotting or even trotting in the flows by lock gates.

Make no mistake: nowadays, canals aren't so tough as they once were. These are beautiful waters with virtually uncaught fish. Once you've learned the ways of the canal and where the fish are, you'll have some fabulous times to either share with your mates or have completely to yourself. So I say – enjoy canals for what they are. These are not commercials where you'll catch a hundred pounds of carp. These are beautiful places: fabulous fisheries and often virgin fishing.

INTRODUCTION

If I were pressed to put my finger on exactly what makes canal fishing so special, I would struggle to find a single answer. Perhaps the sheer variety of experience they provide defies any definitive reply. I've had brilliant days and blank days, on canals which were grim, industrial waters and on others which were some of the most beautifully idyllic places you could set eyes on. I've had great sessions catching smaller species; but then again, some of my biggest-ever specimen catches have come from canals. And whatever the conditions, canals offer consistent, sheltered fishing when other waters are flooded or closed.

Perhaps their attraction also starts with a certain nostalgia and the fact that the local towpath formed such an essential part of my own fishing education. It started with push bikes and perch, which were probably the only fish daft enough to be fooled by the naïve antics of schoolboys. Greater success was a long learning-curve. It meant walking further, refining tactics and increasing one's knowledge. Even the small victories meant something. To catch a tidy net of roach and skimmers felt like a huge achievement.

Certain memories stand out clear as daylight over twenty years later. One was the time I attended my first canal match, joining the old heads with my rattling tackle box and a selection of rods and bank sticks held together with elastic bands. Rather than mock, the regulars were helpful and welcoming, treating me as one of their own. To their amazement as much as my own in that first match I caught a string of perch, rudd and eels on the pole to win my section and a ten pound note into the bargain.

You just never quite know what the day will bring on a canal, that much is still true. You simply never stop learning and making new discoveries, and in one sense I pity youngsters raised on today's predictably muddy and overstocked pools.

The keen canal angler develops a deep, personal connection with their local water, which is more than mere nostalgia or accumulated knowledge. I'm not sure how else to express it. My own love-hate relationship with Exeter Ship Canal, for example, spans a quarter of a century. Even today, I retain a childish excitement, never quite sure what the next bite will bring. There are still dog-days but also sessions where just about anything seems possible.

The variety of fishing on my local canals alone is phenomenal, and in the course of a season you might find me there with anything from a long pole to

A colourful net for the author from the Newport Canal, Shropshire.

carp tackle or flyfishing gear. If nothing else I hope that this book shatters any fixed ideas that canal fishing is a narrow discipline. It is as fascinating and varied as you make it.

The same could be said for all of Britain's canals, and I hope that wherever you live you will find helpful tips and great places to fish in these pages. My own travels in compiling the book have taken me the length and breadth of the country, from the Scottish Highlands to Cornwall; from inner city London to the not-so-grim North and the great maze of Midlands canals. My wingman Russ Hilton deserves extra credit here, for he helped me negotiate countless miles of B-roads and 'Bates Motel'-style accommodation with unerring optimism and humour.

A special mention is also due to all the canal enthusiasts, clubs and tackle shops who helped along the way. It was an incredibly uplifting experience. Look beyond the doom and gloom headlines about cormorants and illegal fishing and a very different picture emerges: in the majority of cases our canals are rich in fish of all types and sizes. Contrary to the fear peddled by our media, we also live in an incredibly friendly country and I found this to be truest in the very places people had told me were 'a bit tasty'. We didn't find any folks warmer, funnier or more welcoming than on the towpaths of Glasgow and Birmingham.

Above all else, my travels were a reminder that as well as being a deep part of our history, canals are also very much a part of our present. Perhaps it's time anglers shouted a little louder about these places. In terms of value, variety and sheer consistency canals offer something far beyond what we modestly refer to as 'bread and butter' fishing. See you on the towpath!

ACKNOWLEDGEMENTS

Perhaps the only list in this book longer than the selection of canals is the sheer number of people to whom I owe a huge debt of gratitude. The more I think about it, the more it seems that the story of canal fishing embraces a huge community which spans everyone from the small boy I lent some maggots on the Monmouth and Brecon, to 81-year-old Alan Smallman on the Newport Canal. I have countless helpful tackle shops and fishing clubs to thank – and can only hope this book supports you in some small way, as you support this great sport of ours.

As for key individuals, I would first like to mention Russ Hilton for his dedication, enthusiasm and company. Merlin, Karen and Jo at Merlin Unwin Books for their unerring support. My parents, for a thousand lifts down to the canal while I was growing up. Steve Stones, for your encouragement and support. All at the *Angling Times*, for help with canal records and unusual archive material. John Harding, from the Waterway Wanderers scheme. Tom Balaam for his ace photography skills. Tony Keeling, for your brilliant facts and enthusiasm on canals. Dan Sales, Des Taylor and John Cheyne for adding their wisdom and catches to these pages. Steve Partner, for film work as well as backing me through the hard times. Jeff Hatt for his invaluable work on tracking down canal record fish. Barry Fisher, Dave Giddy, Steve Lockett, Paul Hamilton and all at *The Anglers Arms* for your help and humour. Steve Sutton and David Stevens, for your brilliant canal anecdotes and pictures. And a big shout out to many other anglers for their assistance and friendship (I'm bound to have missed someone, but I appreciate every one of you!): Norbert Darby, Dave Sellick, Ian Nadin, Will Barnard, Chris Lambert, Pete Gregory, Steve Moore, Seb Nowosiad, Will Smith, Roly Palmer, Zac Newton, Peter Higgins, Tyrone Norah, Adam Moxey, Bob James, Pete Wilkins, Ray Minty, David Overland, Alan Smallman, Peter Wardle, Andy Mytton.

PICTURE CREDITS

I wish to specially thank: Tom Balaam 16, 23, 24, 54, 123, 128, 199, 200, 203, 204; Will Barnard 167; James Callison 100; John Garnett 106; Pete Gregory 99, 109, 122, 155, 173; Russ Hilton 7, 21, 42, 58, 64, 65, 90, 132, 140, 142, 210; Darren Ketteringham 82, 131; Steve Lockett 47; Frazer McBain 52, 67; Ian Nadin 147; Dan Sales 68, 80, 87, 166, 168, 218; Steve Sutton 202, 203; Des Taylor 4, 64, 91. Alex Garnett for his diagram artwork.

Additional thanks to:

London Canal Museum for archive pictures, 10, 11, 171; Wrexham County Borough Council for images of the Pontcysyllte Aqueduct 13, 191; Scottishcanals.co.uk for images of the Forth and Clyde Canal and Falkirk Wheel.

A Brief History of CANALS

Walking along a sunny towpath, it is easy to forget that the rise of Britain's vast canal network was nothing to do with leisure, but has its roots in heavy industry. It takes us to an age of hardship when trains and modern highways were not even a pipe dream. The transportation of goods and materials across the nation demanded a better solution than the muddy, rutted roads in existence.

To industrial tycoons, man-made waterways made perfect sense. They allowed greater loads to be carried in a smoother, more reliable manner. Perhaps not surprisingly, the potteries of the Midlands were among the keenest early advocates of a system far less prone to smashing up their wares. Man-made alterations and extensions to existing waterways can be charted right back many centuries, but 'canal fever' only really exploded in the 18th century. In a frenzy of new schemes, everything from textiles to tobacco began to be shifted by horse-drawn barges, with the new waterways forming the very arteries of British prosperity.

Navvies dug and drank like it was going out of fashion; whole networks of canals sprang up; towns grew and chimneys belched with the smoke of an increased fuel supply. The moneymen rubbed their hands as the waters teemed with commerce. Better still, in the quieter moments amidst the din of industry, the nation's anglers discovered that fish from neighbouring waterways were quick to colonise these channels. Moreover, they brought the gentle art of fishing closer to home for countless citizens. Sunday afternoons would never be the same again.

Dawn of the Navvies

Long before any mechanical digging machinery, canals were dug by hand. This was the role of the 'navvy' (short for 'navigator'), a term for those working to create navigable waterways. These rugged men, often migrant workers from Ireland, travelled in gangs looking for work. It was backbreaking, dangerous labour. Come rain or snow, they could be seen attacking projects with picks and shovels or even gunpowder, using horses and wheelbarrows to take away tons of stone and earth.

A little like modern carp anglers, they would camp by the sides of a canal in all the seasons. They were the toughest of the tough, with calloused hands, weather-beaten faces and even the odd missing limb. On occasion, canal banks would collapse and navvies would be crushed to death or buried alive. They also had

Narrowboats became family homes, as well as conveyors of goods.

a reputation for recklessness and when the working day was done, they loved nothing more than a spot of drinking, whoring and fighting.

The slang term 'Cut' (literally referring to a newly-cut channel) comes from the days of the navvy. Each new digging was then lined with wet clay known as 'puddle'. To make it watertight, navvies would pack down the clay with their own feet, or even by driving sheep or cattle along the canal.

Literally hundreds of thousands of navvies were responsible for Britain's canals. The Manchester Ship Canal alone, one of the last to be dug, required 16,000 of these hardy souls. It seems hard to imagine today, but many of our most tranquil waters were founded on the blood, sweat and hard graft of these men. Even a half-mile section of canal required huge amounts of labour. You wouldn't have wanted to argue with one, nor pick up his bar tab, but we owe a huge debt to the navvies.

Rise and Fall

The period between 1770-1840 is regarded as the 'Golden Age' of canals for good reason. The technological advancement of the nation was studded with phenomenal

BRITAIN'S EARLIEST CANAL?

The site of the nation's first 'Cut' is a subject that gets rival tourist boards hot under the collar, and there are at least two main contenders. The Bridgewater Canal, so instrumental in the growth of Manchester as an industrial powerhouse, is thought to be the first, opened in 1761. Northern Ireland's Newry Canal is older, however, opened in 1742.

In terms of waters adapted or cut as navigation channels, Exeter Ship Canal dates back much further, to the 1560s, while strictly speaking the Romans also created channels such as Foss Dyke for similar purposes. Perhaps we'd better let the tourist boards fight this one out.

works of ingenuity such as aqueducts and sophisticated lock systems. Things were looking good, and not only did the new waterways drive huge industrial progress, they changed the lives of thousands of water-users. An unprecedented number of workers and their families began to live on boats and waterside dwellings, creating whole new communities. Canals became not simply a means to an end, but a deeply significant part of the British landscape.

If the wealthy Victorian developers can be credited for the rise and rise of our canals however, they also contributed to their demise. The development of railways spelt the beginning of the end for canals, at least in terms of economic viability. Trains could carry incredible loads at far greater speeds. And whereas across Europe many canals were widened and improved

Top: Barges depart from London, crammed with goods and materials.

Middle: for generations of urban children, canals have been an introduction to nature.

Bottom: Canals were the motorways of their era and only declined with the advent of the steam train.

Leonardo da Vinci was the first to draw plans of the 'mitre' gate, that came to be used as the standard lock gate worldwide.

to carry ships with much larger cargoes, UK developers were reluctant to go down that route – partly because the magnates who owned the canals were the same rich boys now pumping money into rail.

The writing was on the lock gates, you might say. The picture-book canals of the British countryside were built for narrowboats, not the huge vessels you might find in Rotterdam or Copenhagen, and without improvements, decline was inevitable. Some slowed down, others were rendered virtually derelict over the years. Various on-going canal projects were never completed – which is why at various places in the British countryside, canals seem to peter out aimlessly and unfinished. Some sit there in picturesque isolation; other weedy swamps barely figure on maps.

Rebirth

If we owe the birth of the canals to the vision of wealthy industrialists and the graft of the navvies, we owe their revival, and in many cases their very salvation, to leisure and conservation groups. The authorities who labelled derelict waters as a blot on the landscape were in many cases ready for drastic solutions, until locals made their true feelings known.

The British love canals, or at least have learned to love them. Once the clang of commerce had died down, we began to see them not as places of toil, but play. Boating, cycling, country walks and, yes, fishing, became favourite pastimes of a

The Bonded Warehouse, Dudley: a reminder of Britain's industrial past.

prosperous nation with more leisure time than ever before.

On an ever-more crowded island, canals seem to have found an even higher value with public use. Problems aside, you might even describe the current age as something of a renaissance. The battle cry across counties nationwide is no longer 'Fill it in!' but 'Save our local Cut!'

In fishing terms, our canal network represents arguably Britain's most vast, untapped fishing resource. There are over 2,000 miles of canal still in existence, controlled by a huge number of angling clubs. The Birmingham area alone has more canals than Venice.

Feats of Wonder

- **The Standedge Tunnel** on the Huddersfield Narrow Canal would take a ridiculous amount of 'legging it'. At three miles it is the longest, deepest canal tunnel in the UK.
- **The Falkirk Wheel** *(see page 23)* is a more modern feat of wonder, opened in 2002. Linking the Forth and Clyde to the Union Canal, it is a unique, rotating boat lift. The only one of its kind, the wheel stands at 24 metres high, as tall as an eight-storey building.
- **The Pontcysyllte Aqueduct**, which carries the Llangollen canal over the valley of the river Dee, is still widely regarded as one of the most magnificent feats of engineering in Britain's industrial history. Standing at 38.4 metres with a spectacular nineteen spans, it was the world's tallest aqueduct for some 200 years.

The Pontcysyllte Aqueduct, near Wrexham: once the world's tallest aqueduct.

Trivia

Legging it *A phrase now used for making a speedy, and often dodgy, getaway, has its origins on the narrowboats of Britain's canals. When boats passed under tunnels, horses could not use the towpaths, so crews had to lie on their backs on top of vessels and literally 'leg it' through, using their feet on the sides and roof of the passage.*

Unusual Cargoes

As well as the more common fuels and raw materials, canals were also used to transport a range of stranger cargoes:

Gunpowder

In some areas barges once carried gunpowder, perhaps in the hope that the smooth transit on water might prevent accidents. Not so in 1874, when a convoy of barges was rocked with explosions beside London's Regent's Park.

Ice

Before the electrical age, ice was imported from Norway in huge quantities and supplied via canal to fishmongers, dairies and hospitals. In 1857 alone, London ice tycoon Carlo Gatti shifted 400 tons.

Paupers

Sometimes barges also carried human traffic, such as poor migrants en route to a new life, heading for ports such as Liverpool.

With miles of water on offer, it pays to be mobile. Just ask Alan Smallman, who still puts a bicycle to good use on the Newport Canal at 81 years young.

CANAL CRAFT

When you consider that over half the British population live within five miles of a canal, it's a curious fact that so few of us are even aware of the hidden world these waterways represent. In a sense this is precisely the charm of canal fishing. Even the most mundane, urban-looking channel is a mystery waiting to be solved.

Canals are anything but predictable. When compared to modern commercial fisheries, they represent a refreshing angling challenge. In place of convenient, well-trodden swims, we are often met with miles of water to explore, much of it seldom fished. A successful day is not a case of simply finding a space to sit down and bait up; it requires thought and effort. It is this learning process, and the potential for exciting, untapped fishing, that makes canal fishing so deeply rewarding.

The Typical Canal?

While it's true that all canals have certain similarities, a look at different waters across the country would quickly reveal a huge diversity of habitats. Some are found in quiet, rural locations where clear, weedy water allows the angler to spot fish at leisure; others are far murkier affairs, churned up by regular boat traffic, where fish cannot easily be located by sight. Some canals are littered with lock gates, bays and bends; others are largely featureless. The bottom can vary from gravel or clay to thick silt.

The varying depths and dimensions of different waters would further defy attempts to describe the 'average' or 'typical' canal. At the top end of the scale are ship canals. These can be over ten feet deep and many metres wide to accommodate huge seagoing vessels. But far more common are the smaller, much shallower canals of around ten to thirteen metres width, designed to take the classic canal barges or 'narrowboats'. These tend to be no more than five or six feet deep even slap bang in the central 'track' of the canal. In secluded locations free of regular boat traffic, silt and debris might render some areas as shallow as a mere two to three feet; enough water to hold fish nonetheless.

Perhaps the most obvious question to any angler looking at a canal they have yet to fish is: 'Where do I start?' The answer often lies in a pair of walking boots and polarising glasses rather than a fishing rod. In morning or evening you may spot fish topping or rolling. There could well be locals fishing and happy to chat. Treat everyone in a friendly, considerate manner and you'll find most regulars helpful. There are also a whole series of useful starting points in the reference section at the end of this book. We can't lead you by the hand or bait the swim for you, but there are productive locations for virtually every canal. Fishing clubs and tackle shops are also listed. Both are a mine of useful information, but they also need your support. So as well as asking questions, be sure to buy a day ticket or dip into your wallet, even if it's just a pint of maggots or some spare hooks.

Most canals have their known 'hot spots' or areas that are match fished. Competition results and typical catches are often archived online, along with the many blogs and articles that a quick internet search will yield. Applications such as Google Earth are also handy. Bear in mind however that even in the age of digital information, you will only scratch the surface looking at a screen.

There is no substitute for getting out on the bank yourself. Look for anything different, interesting or unusual, whether this is a sweeping bend, a wide turning bay, submerged trees and bushes, a lock pool or a place where the canal meets a river or another channel. For the angler who is prepared to explore, the list is endless.

Canals are often underfished waters and the most rewarding experience of all is discovering your own hot spot, which could be an area that seldom sees another angler. Perhaps this is why the fish you catch are likely to be in fantastic condition.

Contrary to appearances, boats do not always spoil the fishing. Sometimes a passing vessel can actually improve sport, while static craft are often holding areas.

Key areas on the canal

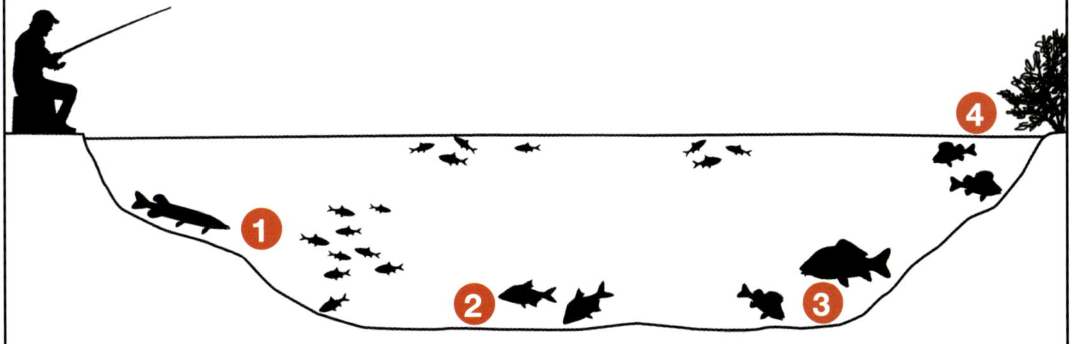

1 Near-margin and shelf: Don't assume you have to reach the far bank to catch fish on a canal. The bottom of the near-shelf is an excellent place to start fishing, where you'll likely find roach and skimmers. Even the shallow water may contain fish such as gudgeon, rudd and pike, especially if there is some cover close in.

2 Central 'Track': The main channel is the deepest part of the canal. Boat traffic also helps to keep it clear and open. Many species are found here, but bream especially like the deep track. During the winter, or when the canal level drops or the water becomes very clear, more fish move towards the middle of the canal for the warmth and safety which deeper water provides. On neglected canals this also rings true, where the only deep water might be right in the middle.

3 Bottom of far-shelf: This is a key area for 'bonus fish' of all kinds, including tench and carp. As with the near-shelf, natural food as well as the bait you introduce tends to gather here. Plumb the depth carefully here, to find the deepest point of the slope.

4 Far-margin: Sometimes fish will be found right on the far bank of canals, particularly if the water is coloured or there is some cover. Species such as perch, chub and carp particularly love far-bank features, the more pronounced the better.

Different Types of Canal

There is no such a thing as the 'typical' canal. Each one is unique and there is no substitute for gathering your own experience on a water. That said, we can certainly identify a few 'types' of canal that provide a useful general model. This is not set in stone. For example, some individual canals will be quite varied in themselves – combining busy urban sections and quieter, clearer locations along their course.

Knowing how to recognize different types of water and deal with different conditions are all part of the craft of canal fishing; and with no closed season on most towpaths, you'll certainly witness great variation each year.

Rural canals can be clear and weedy, offering seclusion as well as a different fishing challenge.

Busy, Coloured Canals

Although quiet anglers might be forgiven for wishing they had the canal all to themselves, the reality is that these are shared waterways. On many Cuts, regular boat traffic keeps the water fairly coloured, stirring up the bottom sediment. Don't take this as bad news however! Boats keep the main channel free of weed, while the extra colour in the water can actually make the fish feed more confidently. They will also feel safer venturing into shallower water – and boat traffic can also make them more inclined to hold close to the shelves on either side of the canal.

Perhaps the biggest surprise on many canals is just how rich they are in life. The most urban locations imaginable can be stuffed full of fish, and species such as roach, perch and carp thrive in distinctly man-made environments. As an angler, you can deliver the perfect response to every passer-by who asks that timelessly bloody stupid question: 'Are there really any fish in there?'

You won't be able to fish by sight very often on such canals. In the warmer months you might spot fish like carp and rudd on the surface, but the rest of the time, the angler is essentially fishing blind and using their judgement. They must use other clues, such as bubbling or rolling fish, and also look for any attractive features. Nor is there any rule to say you must remain rooted to the spot. Where visible clues are few, it can be well worth trying an hour or so in several spots until you find the fish.

Where boat traffic can suddenly appear and lock gates crank open, the stillest water can start to 'tow' through, so

Little & Often

The 'little and often' rule is a good one for feeding bait on most canals, but especially so where boats regularly pass and churn up the bottom, dispersing your bait in the process. Instead of baiting up heavily, try doing so more gradually, adding a small ball of groundbait or pouch of maggots every few minutes. Do the same every time a boat or two pass, to concentrate the fish again.

the angler must be adaptable. This might mean changing the depth to cope with a new influx of water (canals can rise or drop several inches while you're fishing!) or switching to a heavier, more stable float rig.

Light angling pressure often means beautifully-conditioned fish.

Boats are by no means the curse some of us take them for. Creatures such as bloodworm and shrimp are stirred up when boats pass, prompting fish to feed. Predators will sometimes use the temporary commotion to go on the attack.

Fish know exactly what boats are. Moored vessels, especially those which are lived on or static for days on end, are often real havens for fish – and this is especially true where predators such as cormorants patrol. You should avoid casting heavy leads or firing bait close to boats however – the pole is a much safer way to fish and feed bait, or you could even try clipping your line and making gentle underarm casts. Above all, it is vital for anglers and boat users to get along in harmony: both parties benefit.

Birds can offer further canal clues. Where locals feed them, you can be sure roach and bream will also find bread.

Seasonal variations also come into play on busy canals too. Holiday periods can be hectic unless you plan to fish at the crack of dawn or into evening. But even the busiest waterway will slow down in the winter, when the water often clears and tactics change again. Other methods such as bread punch and lure fishing come to the fore as clarity improves. The fish will also shoal tighter and seek out deep and sheltered spots, making bumper catches possible if you can find them.

Sometimes your best canal fishing assets are your eyes and feet. Polarising glasses also help you spot fish. Above: this basking pike could easily have gone unnoticed.

Clear, Weedy Canals

In complete contrast to busy, muddy-looking waterways, Britain is also blessed with some glorious open countryside and canals every bit as pretty as rivers. This can be down to the simple fact that the water may no longer be navigable by boats. Such canals are beautiful, if sometimes overgrown places.

It always makes me smile when I hear clear, overgrown waters described as 'unfishable'. This is very rarely the case and in fact these waters represent some of the richest habitats of all. Clear water and an abundance of natural food equate to healthy fish in superb condition. Roach, rudd, tench and pike do especially well in such conditions.

There are particular challenges to fishing wilder canals. Not least of all is the weed. The angler might have to get stuck into a cramped, overgrown swim or even clear some space. They might even need to bring a weed rake to cut a pitch for fishing. Tactics also change.

Besides abundant weed, silt can be thick on wild, neglected waters which are often the shallowest of all canals. Legering for any species can be rendered impractical, with float tackle much preferred. Baits must also be chosen carefully. Offerings such as bread that will fall slowly and not sink into the vegetation or silt are useful, while dead baits, worms and boilies can be popped up so the fish can still easily find them.

Catches can vary greatly – as a puzzled author demonstrates on the Sheffield & Tinsley.

With visibility so superb, these waters also make excellent places to try alternative tactics. Free-lined baits such as floating crust are exciting and effective in weedy swims. Lure fishing also works excellently in clear water, although floating or even weedless lures might be the most practical solution. Last but not least, the fly rod is a delightful alternative where the water is clear and invertebrate life abundant. This is especially true on warm summer days when a small dark dry or slow sinking wet fly can be excellent for rudd, roach and chub.

It can be fantastic fun just watching the fish on a wild, clear canal, but new challenges also come into play. The fish will find it much easier to spot the angler, hence spooking them becomes an issue. Stalking the banks quietly and carefully can be important, using any bankside cover to conceal one's presence. Sunny, still days in particular can be a test of stealth, where putting a shadow over the water or making a clumsy cast could easily scare the fish.

Dominic's Tip

WINTER MEASURES

When does a frosty canal become unfishable? Enterprising anglers still catch by breaking the ice, but such extreme action is not always required. Areas such as inflows, marinas and urban sections are often slightly warmer, making them good winter holding areas and less prone to freezing over.

This intimate style of fishing can be truly thrilling however and being able to watch and cast to visible fish is a huge advantage. Since we are no longer fishing blind, the bigger fish are also easier to single out.

Russ Hilton plays a good fish at the edge of a turning bay, a classic area to find bream and other good-sized fish.

Larger Canals

When discussing the main types of canal, another aspect that can vary greatly is their size and depth. As well as the narrow, cute little channels, Britain has some much larger beasts such as the Gloucester, Exeter and Manchester Ship canals designed to take sea-going vessels.

The sheer scale of such waters can represent a daunting challenge. With much greater depths to contend with, methods such as long pole, feeder and specialist legering techniques come to the fore. The same rules of finding features and accurately assessing the depth still apply however.

Perhaps the biggest problem on ship canals is finding, or intercepting, the fish in the first place where there is simply more water for them to hide. For specimen anglers, pre-baiting is a good ploy, so long as you have done the groundwork and found a promising spot or two. The more occasions you can do this before fishing, the better, and introducing bait into two or three areas is a more failsafe idea than putting all your hopes in one location.

Taking on a hulking great ship channel is probably no place to begin your canal fishing career. For those who persevere, however, the biggest canals are capable of producing some huge fish. Large carp, bream and pike thrive here, including fish that would smash the current canal records.

Night Fishing

It takes a brave soul to stay out on a canal through darkness hours, but the rewards can be well worth the effort.

Carp, eels and zander are especially active after dark and the other advantage is that boats are absent (it is illegal in many areas for boats to operate at night).

DEPTH CONTROL

For any style of canal fishing, getting an accurate feel for depths is important. They might look uniform, but many canals are greatly varied in this respect. Neglected areas can be deceptively shallow, for example, while average depths can sharply increase around locks, bridges and moorings. Time spent plumbing and making mental notes is never wasted.

A weighted lure or lead can be useful, but a float is the most accurate way to test the depth. Some canals have thick silt, in which case an extra-light plummet or split shot (or even a 'snow shoe' style version with some mesh glued to the base to lie flat and avoid digging in) will give a more accurate reading. For shy biting fish there is no substitute for accuracy.

We've already mentioned the 'shelf' on each side of the canal, and these should be investigated thoroughly. On some venues you will find a pronounced slope; on others, especially those that are well silted, you'll find a much more gentle gradient more like the sides of a shallow bowl.

Common sense and careful organization are the watchwords of the night angler. You must keep off the towpath and be prepared for any eventuality.

Urban Fishing

Contrary to appearances, some of the most underexploited of all canal fishing occurs in town and city centres. Salford Quays and the canals of Birmingham are just two areas that contain good stocks of fish. Whether you brave some of the tougher spots for a cast is your decision, but a few simple rules make sense. Firstly, pick your times carefully. Early morning at first light is often preferable to evenings, when dodgy types and drunks

The ultimate urban canal feature – the remarkable Falkirk Wheel on the Forth & Clyde Canal, one of the most important coarse fisheries in Scotland.

Appearances can be deceptive on urban canals, which are often full of fish of all species.

roam towpaths. It is always good policy to take a friend and avoid leaving anything valuable on show; this includes your most prized tackle! Scale down your gear and keep a low profile, and you could be in for a big surprise. Perhaps the easiest methods for really 'tasty' urban locations are lure fishing and stalking, hit-and-run-style methods. Snags can be a menace too however, so single hook lures, and rigs where leads will come free in the event of snagging, can be invaluable.

Certain species do especially well in urban locations. Huge perch and carp, for example, thrive around boats and man-made structures. Species such as roach and bream also love deep spots such as boatyards and basins. As well as the extra depth, town and city centres

Weed cutting is carried out on a rural waterway: some maintenance is vital, but at the same time those rich, weedy waters branded as 'unfishable' by lazy anglers can offer outstanding sport.

also offer sheltered, slightly warmer water, making them especially attractive to fish seeking sanctuary in the winter.

A Captive Audience?

Finding concentrations of fish is one of the primary objectives of the canal angler in what could be miles of similar-looking water. This can take some investigation, but certain scenarios do crop up time and again.

As well as long, unbroken sections of water, many canals have shorter areas enclosed by lock gates (sometimes called

It doesn't get much more urban than central London, but there are still fish to be caught.

'pounds'). Because they are self-contained waters in effect, these are often consistent places to find fish. Clubs will also often stock areas like this, knowing full well that the fish will not wander miles. The Newport, Sankey, Grand Union and Dudley Number One are just four examples of canals with such 'pounds'.

In other areas a similar situation arises where the local Cut has been drastically closed off or shortened to just a few hundred yards of water. Such waters are also ripe for stocking and often contain fish such as carp, crucians and even ide. Not strictly traditional, you might say, but fishing tends to be consistent and baits such as pellets and sweetcorn will often work as well as maggots and casters.

Another factor that helps concentrate fish is the influence of local anglers. Where regular matches are held or pleasure anglers congregate, the frequent introduction of bait will keep fish in the area. Predators will also follow, and the opportunist pike angler can cash in by fishing just after a match ends while the pike pick off slightly dazed fish released after the weigh-in.

Winter fishing can also be rewarding, although fish tend to cluster, favouring deeper water.

COMPETITION

TACKLE

If canals themselves present a huge variety of settings and species, the same is true of the equipment found on towpaths nationwide. You could spend a small fortune and still not cover every base. That said, it is also possible to target a range of canal fish at a very modest cost.

My own exploits on the local Cut began with a four-metre fibreglass whip. It was hardly state-of-the-art, even in the Eighties. It featured pointless yellow markings on the handle, and a decent perch or surprise eel would cause the whole thing to plunge over, to my great excitement. I was immensely proud of this telescopic weapon, which in terms of sheer numbers of fish caught would probably be the best value item of tackle I have ever owned.

These days the boot of my car might contain anything from overnight carping supplies to a fly rod. These are at the far ends of the spectrum however and for much of the time, a canal angler's staple would be a pole or light match rod.

Other sundries and items for the canal angler are many – and we'll dip into a few of these shortly. Beyond a rod, something to sit on and a landing net, the rest can be accumulated at your leisure.

Whips

Shorter poles, or 'whips' are an ideal tool for catching fish at short range on any canal. Most are telescopic and tend to be cheap, although you could fork out many times the cash for a beautifully light, top class model. Used with a simple float rig the same length as the pole itself, they represent true simplicity. With no reel to

Dominic's Tip

Cheaper whips are a great starting point for the canal, but many have pretty dodgy tips. If this is the case, an excellent solution is to carefully remove the very end of the tip and glue on a stonfo-style sliding connector; these are reliable and a really easy way to attach your rigs via a loop knot.

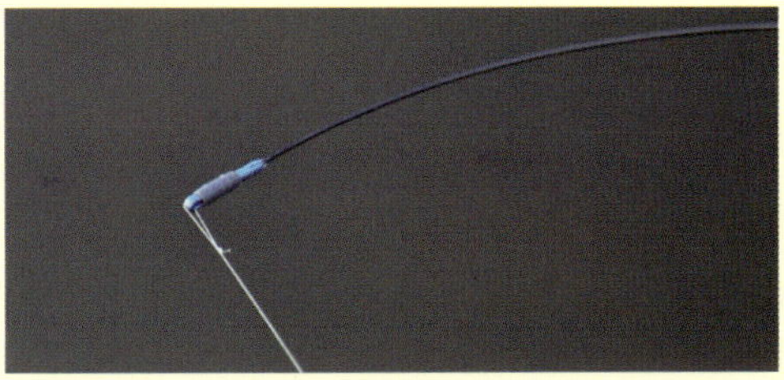

tangle, they are also ideal for youngsters and novices. That said, some of our finest anglers also use whips to fish with total control at close quarters, catching fish like roach, perch, gudgeon and bleak at incredible speed.

Most fish are swung to hand with the whip. Larger samples require a landing net. These short poles will handle fish like bream, but bigger surprises can lead to problems. Whip fishing is fun, light-line fishing. With a few rigs set up on winders, you can be fishing within seconds. Lines are seldom greater than 3lb breaking strain, often lighter.

Poles

If ever a piece of fishing equipment was tailor-made for canal fishing, it must be the long pole. The advantages they offer in terms of accuracy, control and finesse are huge. Nor are they just for small fish or match anglers – these days, poles are cheaper and stronger than ever. A model of 11-13 metres will hit the far bank of most canals with deadly precision. For the lowdown on pole choices, rigs and techniques, see the dedicated chapter on p127.

A multi-section carbon pole is the perfect weapon for canal fishing.

Towpath Etiquette

KEEPING TIDY ON THE TOWPATH

With cyclists, dog walkers and joggers, canals can be hazardous places for delicate items of tackle. Always keep your kit tidy and lay items such as pole sections parallel to the bank, rather than sticking out onto the towpath. Another good trick to make passers-by wary of your kit is to place a tougher, less valuable item, such as a net bag, sticking out slightly behind you, so bikes and boots take a wider berth.

Float Rods

Often known as 'match' rods, the ideal blank to float fish on canals is something well-balanced, light and fine in the tip. A fairly fine model will cast small floats with ease and allow the use of light hooklengths. Just as importantly, such a tool will give you a great deal of pleasure even if the fish are modest-sized.

Although many float rods come in a length of 12-13ft, canal anglers often drop down to a shorter model of eleven or even ten feet – a slightly more compact

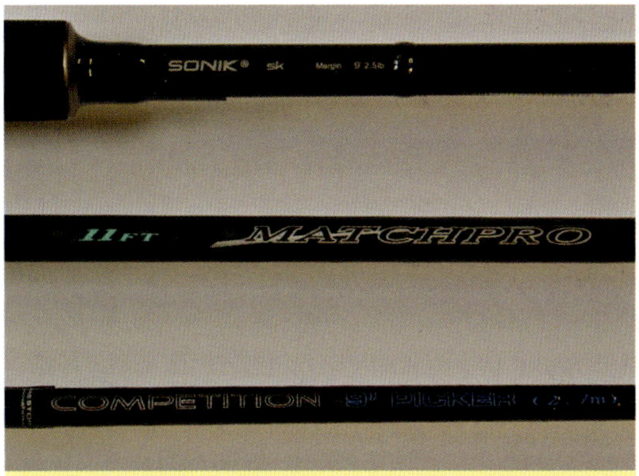

Rods vary greatly on towpaths, but for canal fishing, shorter, lighter tools are often more suitable – and fun – to use.

rod is great fun and well-suited to smaller canals. Nor does such a weapon always come second best to the pole; in the winter, for example, when waters go very clear and fish are wary, a light waggler can be preferable to a pole tip waving over their heads.

Feeder Rods

It is perhaps only on the bigger, deeper canals, or on wide sections such as turning bays and boat yards where a feeder rod becomes a popular tool for the Cut angler. That said, a tip rod can be a useful plan B when the elements make float fishing impractical, and the feeder is an excellent tactic for bream and tench.

As with float rods, the 12ft-plus models tend to be a little overgunned for all but the widest expanses of water. A more appropriate tool would often be a little wand of a rod, sometimes called a 'picker', measuring 8-10ft. These offer terrific accuracy for casting little feeders and bombs, as well as lot of fun playing small-to-medium-sized fish. Look for a light model with a choice of push-in tips – a delicate option is a must for roach and skimmers.

Specimen & Carp Rods

An increasingly common sight on towpaths are specialist rods for fish like carp and pike, as more anglers seem to have cottoned on to the fact that canals contain some excellent-sized fish. Where carp are concerned, your usual tackle for the species will suffice. Rods of 3lb test curve are rather heavy, however, so I often prefer a more forgiving blank of around 2lb test. Long-distance casting is seldom an issue; even a 3oz lead and solid PVA bag can be swung accurately to the far bank with such a tool on most canals. A more forgiving action also makes for less risk of breakages and hook pulls with hard-fighting fish at close quarters. Another development has been the introduction of shorter blanks of just 10ft or so – and these can be handy in cramped swims.

Where pike are concerned, you can also go for blanks a little lighter than the standard 3lb test curve rod for bait fishing, which won't provide much fight from the average jack. A 2-2½lb test blank is more fun – or you could even try a spinning rod. I would always keep mainlines and traces heavy, however. Anything less than 15lb mono or braid is irresponsible and won't buy you any extra bites.

Less numerous in the pages of tackle catalogues are those lighter specimen rods of 1-1½lb and a half test curve. These are superb for fish like zander, bream and perch, which are easily bumped off the hook with overly powerful rods.

Finally, you will also find a wide range of rods for fishing with lures on canals. These are covered in my chapter on lure fishing, along with the different types of artificial baits for canal predators.

Balanced Tackle

Whichever species you target, the golden rule is to use balanced tackle. Often this will mean kit which is rather lighter than standard gear. Canal fishing is often about finesse, and finer rods allow the use of lighter tackle with less risk of breakages.

Fly Tackle

The fly angler is an increasingly common sight on the local Cut. In fact I kick myself these days whenever I find a clear canal and have no fly rod in the car. Two favourite set-ups come out to play time and again in my case: a 10ft 3-4 weight rod and reel is delightful for targeting roach, rudd and chub. Such a blank allows beautifully delicate presentation with a floating line. Shorter rods are also fun, but I find the ten footer gives much better control around bankside growth and snags.

Pike are perhaps the most popular fly quarry of all on canals but here you'll need a rod with some backbone. Huge flies and heavy rods are in most cases totally unnecessary however and I find an eight weight set-up perfect; very sporty for jacks, but strong enough to land a surprise double. A floating line is often all that is required, although I will use a sink tip or switch to a fast intermediate on deep ship canals.

Other options also make for exciting adventures and I've even had tench and bream on nymphs. It is a fascinating challenge and one that cannot be conveyed fully in the limited space of these pages; for further reading, my book *Flyfishing for Coarse Fish* has a great deal of useful information.

Reels

The rule of balanced tackle is your major consideration when picking reels to match your rods. A dinky little fixed spool, capable of holding a hundred yards of 2-3lb line is perfect for a light match or feeder rod. Even for larger canal specimens such as carp and pike, however, reels needn't be huge, and a mid-sized bait-runner capable of holding a hundred yards of 15lb mono or 30lb braid is about the biggest I use.

As with all tackle, it pays to get the best quality reel you can afford. A reliable drag is a must and it never ceases to amaze me how few anglers seem to spend a minute or two setting this to perfection before they fish. The drag should give line well before the line breaks. You can always tighten up during the fight, whereas it's far more difficult to slacken off on a hard-running fish without getting smashed up.

Lines

A great range of fishing lines are involved in canal fishing. Each species chapter will deal with recommended strengths and types. Quality is essential where any lines are concerned. Once you have hooked a good fish, it is too late to do anything about weak or suspect line.

Different lines have very different qualities: floating lines are perfect for waggler fishing, for example, while sinking lines are better for legering. Treating agents such as sprays can also be useful to make your line perform properly, whether you want it to stick crisply to the surface when float fishing, or sink your main line beneath a ripple.

Monofilament lines should be changed at least once each season and regularly inspected. A common fault is to load the reel spool improperly. The line should come only slightly shy (to within 2-3mm) of the edge or 'lip' of the spool. Not only does this aid casting, it also allows you to discard a little line as required while still leaving plenty on the spool. I like to do this on a fairly regular basis, removing the last 3-4ft that have suffered the most wear and tear so I am always using fresh, undamaged line.

Lines for canals range from tough braids to the finest of monofilaments.

Hooklengths Tip

Tying a selection of spare hooklengths is an excellent idea and by keeping a few in identical lengths, you can be back in business quickly after a break, without altering the depth of your float rigs. For newcomers, or those pressed for time, ready-tied hooklengths are another convenient solution.

Rig Lines and Hooklengths

For much canal fishing, sensitive presentation is important and a hooklength (a final, short section of finer line) is important. This not only presents your bait in a subtle manner but prevents tackle loss or, worse still, a tethered fish, should you suffer a break. Modern low diameter lines are perfect for this role. Pre-stretched and electronically tested, these high tech lines are incredibly fine for their high strength. They can be brittle so are unsuitable as reel lines in really fine diameters. Pole rigs are another matter, however, since the elastic provides the stretch to cushion the fight of a larger fish.

The rule of balanced tackle comes into play once again when selecting a hooklength material. A loop-to-loop connection is a strong, simple way to connect hooklengths and the breaking strain of the finer line should be lower, but not vastly different to your main line (for example a 3lb hooklength would be perfect for 4lb reel line). How long should your hooklength be? This also varies. Some match anglers employ tiny hooklengths of 6in or less. But these can be fiddly and somewhere in the region of 10in is more common for float methods, or anything up to 3ft for feeder fishing.

Shots and Smaller Weights

It goes without saying that you require weights to cock your floats. A selection of smaller shot can be vital where canals are concerned, especially where finicky, shy-biting species such as roach and skimmers are concerned. A selection of shot from AAs and BBs will be required for wagglers and larger floats, while tiny shot right down to size 10 and 11s are needed to correctly dot down a fine-bristled pole float.

A range of split shot. For really small sizes, styls or 'stotz' can be a superb alternative.

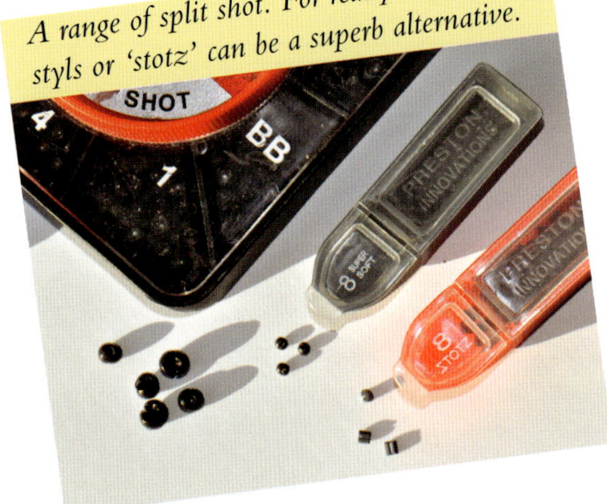

Olivettes are also worth mentioning for pole fishing. These make a tidy, tangle-proof weight for fishing on or near the bottom.

Another good alternative is the use of styls or 'stotz'. These are cylindrical rather than round, and seem to stay put much better than smaller round shot, which can ping off light lines during use.

Old or poor quality weights can damage your line, tend to come off easily and should be avoided at all costs. Go for a reputable make such as Anchor or Dinsmores.

Depth Plumbs

Accurately gauging the depth is an essential part of canal fishing. There is a world of difference between having it 'about right' and absolutely spot-on. A thorough job with a suitable plummet also gives you an impression of the bottom and whether it is silty, hard or weedy.

The problem with many of these weights is that they will plunge into the silt, giving you a measurement that is slightly out. For a more accurate result, go for the lightest depth plumb you can find, or just use a split shot such as an AA pinched next to the hook.

For an accurate reading of depth, opt for the smallest depth plumb you can find – or try a larger split shot.

Dominic's Tip

Once you have the exact depth, a little marker can be added to your rod or pole. A correction fluid pen is ideal for this and means that, should you need to tackle up again, you will still have the correct depth.

Floats

Various floats are used for canal fishing, but by far the most common are pole floats and wagglers. Much larger floats are also used for pike fishing. I discuss all of these in the chapters on specialist methods and species.

A good selection of floats for your chosen method is highly recommended – but you needn't always stick to concrete rules: a sensitive pole float can be used with a long match rod for fishing the near side, for example, while tiny wagglers are also useful for whip fishing.

Bombs, Leads and Swim Feeders

Legering on canals is less popular than float fishing, but when big fish or bigger distances are present, a selection of these items is useful. Feeders of several kinds are an excellent way to deliver bait accurately and regularly into the swim.

Cage feeders leak groundbait fast, making them ideal for shallow waters up to six feet. For deeper water where you want bait only to disperse nearer the bottom, standard groundbait feeders are more suitable. Last but not least, method feeders can also be useful on occasion. These are used with very short hooklengths and sticky groundbait, to encourage a self-hooking effect with fish like bream and carp.

Sizes of feeders can vary, from tiny models to deliver small amounts of feed in winter, to ounce plus models that would suit a wide canal basin on a windy day.

Bombs and leads have their uses too, usually for specimen-style tactics. Carp weights in particular can be confusing, but for most of the time, simple leads are all that are required. The only specialist lead I might be tempted to use for carp would be a slightly flattened design for really silty canals, where you don't want the weight to bury into the bottom too far.

Hooks

A great range of hooks can be applied to canal fishing, with fine wired patterns down to a size 24 at one end, a size 4 treble at the other. I deal with hook sizes in the sections on baits and fish species.

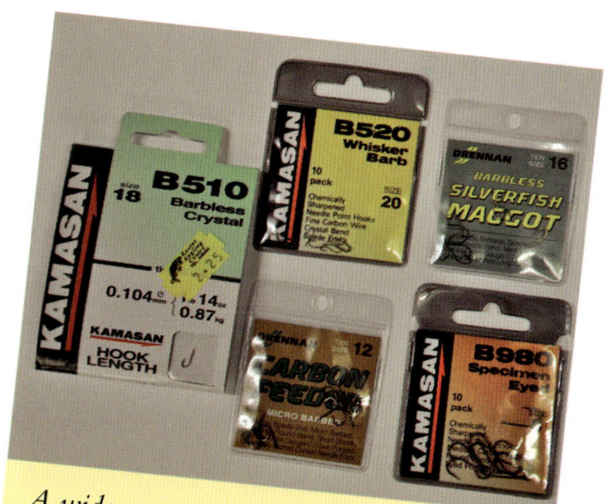

A wide range of hooks are required for canal fishing, from fine-wired maggot versions to forged specimen models.

The same rule applies to hooks as other tackle: buy the best quality you can afford. You can have the best rod in the world, but the hook is your most vital connection.

Eyed hooks are easiest to use, but in smaller sizes many canal anglers prefer spade ends, which sit beautifully straight on the line and arguably have a slight edge in terms of presentation. The best modern hooks are needle sharp but have a high strength even in lighter gauges.

Change hooks

Often overlooked, the hook is the most vital component in any rig. Smaller hooks should be replaced every session. On a hectic day's fishing, match anglers will even freshen up by changing to a new hook part way through the session. Larger hooks, such as those on lures, are well worth running a hook sharpener over when they start to lose their edge.

The choice of whether to go barbed or barbless is yours. I have no aversion to barbless, especially for smaller fish species, although a micro-barb helps when pole fishing, as a barbless one can slip out in that momentary loss of tension as you unhook sections.

Disgorgers

An absolute essential for most general canal fishing, the disgorger is the only reliable way to remove the hook safely from a fish that has taken the bait deeper. Easy to use with practice, you simply keep the line tight, slide the little notch down to the hook and push down.

Regular, micro and large disgorgers are all available, with the smaller heads useful for dainty fish and tiny hooks. I usually buy several at a time because I am excellent at losing the damned things. On the bank, tuck yours in a place it can easily be found, such as in your ground-bait or behind the ear.

Forceps / Long-nosed Pliers

For big hooks and larger species, especially those with teeth such as pike and zander, forceps or pliers are a must. Opt for quality, purpose-made tools – that set in the garage won't do, so invest in a dedicated, foot-long pair.

Landing Nets

A decent quality landing net is not just a means to an end, but a vital aid in landing the better fish you hook. A light-weight 'pan' style net is ideal for small-to-medium-sized fish, in conjunction with a decent length handle.

For the specimen angler, carp or pike demand something larger. To go undergunned is to risk losing a season's best catch. As a general rule, be optimistic when picking your net; it is much better to have a net which is a little too big than too small. Large triangular specimen nets are ideal for static methods, but are not great for very weedy swims or roving sessions. A generous, solid-framed, collapsible net is preferable for roaming the banks in search of bigger fish.

Keepnets

While not absolutely necessary for the pleasure angler, there is something pleasant about seeing what you've caught at the end of a session. A few sensible guidelines apply however. A decent keepnet should be made of soft, fish-friendly material and not be less than 2.5 metres in length. Fish come to little harm provided you extend the net fully (you can do this by stretching the end out with a net handle or pole sections). If there is regular boat traffic it is also much safer to use a long bank stick to stake out the bottom end to prevent collapsing.

Fish should always be lowered, not dropped or thrown, into a keepnet. Responsible anglers also ensure that fish have ample space and, in warm conditions when oxygen levels are low, keepnets should be used only for shorter periods, or not at all. Some species, such as pike and large carp, should never be retained in a keepnet – and indeed many fishing clubs ban this practice.

Unhooking Mats

These are an essential purchase for the specimen angler. They should be wetted when a big fish is placed on one, and a large mat is sensible for long or bulky species like carp and pike. They also come in handy when photographing your catch; placed beneath your prized fish they could make the difference between a soft landing and a fatal drop.

I also like a foldable mat for roving sessions, as they are lighter than a seat but still protect the backside. Last but not least, a damp mat is also a much kinder way to lay out a catch of fish such as bream or tench with no risk of damage.

Seats and Seat Boxes

Without going into vast detail, somewhere to sit comfortably is another requisite fishing item. Collapsible seats come in many guises. Some of the purpose-made fishing chairs are excellent; they should be portable as well as comfy though, so do test these for lightness. A comfortable shoulder strap is another must if you walk any distance to reach your swim.

For long pole fishing there is only one serious choice for the towpath and that is the seat box. These provide not only useful storage, but keep the angler in a comfortable, raised position to handle several metres of pole. The best have legs that adjust to uneven banks, and a wealth of compartments and add-ons. The options are many, but bait waiters and side trays are especially useful to keep you from continually stooping or straining as you reach for your essentials.

Your choice of seat may not be as exciting as the latest rod, but no angler wants back-ache so do pick wisely. Online ordering can be cheap, but nothing beats trying out and buying items at your local tackle shop, whose local advice and personal service can't be matched by any website.

Polarising Glasses

Brilliant for spotting fish and features, polarising glasses are essential for any angler who likes to stalk, lure or fly fish. I simply wouldn't leave home without mine, for any style of fishing. Even when float fishing on a muddy canal, a decent pair will spare you a headache watching for bites in sunny conditions.

Weed Rake

This item of kit is not so common, but highly valued by those in the know. They are usually home-made by fastening two garden rake heads back to back, before attaching a length of chain or strong rope. Thrown and dragged through the swim, this not only clears an area to fish but will also stir up the bottom a treat. Tench fishers find this especially beneficial.

It may be an item you must make yourself, but a weed rake is well worth the effort on weedy canals.

BAITS

In the course of a year on the Cut, a great variety of baits come to the fore. Everything from a tiny squat to a whole sardine has its place. The one necessity is to use the best quality bait you can find. This doesn't mean great expense, but the angler who is prepared to take a little extra care and effort will be rewarded.

Some of the very finest baits cost little: I would be lost without a simple white loaf of bread or a handful of worms from the compost heap. Others come at a higher premium, but more than repay their expense when it comes to catching fish.

Maggots catch many different species, whatever the season.

Maggots

An invaluable, year-round staple, maggots catch most species of fish. If you had to pick just one bait for canals, maggots would probably top the list. They can be readily bought, easily prepared and even flavoured.

Storage is a sticking point in many households, but maggots will last at least a week in the fridge. They can be cold stored for longer still in a sealed, airtight bag; in this state they go torpid, but do require some air every couple days if you want to keep them in decent condition. Most maggots will come by the pint in sawdust. You can use them like this, but a better idea is to riddle off the dust before fishing. You could also then substitute a different medium: flour keeps them soft, or you could flavour them with some turmeric or, my favourite, a handful of dry groundbait.

Maggots are best used on smallish hooks:

- size 20-22 for a single grub
- size 14-18 for doubles
- size 10-12 for a bunch

Nick them onto the hook finely through just the skin of the blunt end to retain plenty of wriggle. In pairs, they are best hooked back to back. Commonly available in white, red or bronze, a pint

Maggot Tips

DEAD, FLOATING, FLAVOURED… THE POSSIBILITIES ARE ENDLESS

Smart anglers pull off all sorts of tricks with maggots. They can be killed by freezing or immersing in boiling water and in this state won't wriggle into the silt; ideal for when you want them to stay put for longer periods when targeting bream, tench and eels. Another good trick is to keep a separate container of water or fizzy pop. A few minutes in this solution and you have floating maggots, brilliant for counterbalancing your hook and catching roach and rudd on the drop, or indeed legered presentations where you don't want your hookbait disappearing into the weed.

of 'mixed' is a sensible option from the tackle shop; sometimes the fish show a preference for one colour.

Pinkies

Smaller than normal maggots, pinkies come into their own for canal fishing. The beauty of these smaller grubs is that you can trickle more of them into the swim without overfeeding the fish. They keep as well as maggots and can be conditioned the same way. When 'scratching' for bites in tough conditions, they are simply brilliant on tiny hooks, sizes 20-24. You'll also often find pinkies dyed in a bright orange besides the usual colours, and a single 'disco' pinkie on a tiny hook is the sort of bait that will get bites on the most gruelling of days. Don't be deceived by their size however – many a quality bream has been taken on double pinkie.

THE MAGIC OF TINY BAITS

Pinkies and squats are fantastic baits for several reasons. They are incredible value firstly. Even if you feed them every minute, a pint goes a long way. Both are excellent for small fish, but you'll also draw bigger fish and catch these on tiny hookbaits too. Squats come into their own when waters become clear and the fishing hard. Pinkies stand out more and become the better bait when the water is more coloured. There's nothing stopping you from combining baits, and one economical trick is to ask for a pinch of pinkies with your pint of squats, or a few big maggots with your pint of pinkies so you have a few bigger hook samples.

Squats

The tiniest of maggots, squats, come in a fine sand and require rather more careful storage than other grubs. They can be stored on the cool floor of a garage for short periods, but keep the temperature control at a higher setting if you wish to store them in the fridge.

Squats come into their own for winter fishing, when they possess a terrific ability to hold fish like roach and skimmers in the swim. Because they are so tiny, they keep the fish interested for ages without filling them up. They work well with groundbait and unlike bigger maggots they won't break up balls of the stuff. They also make good winter hook-baits on tiny hooks. I also like squats in conjunction with liquidized bread; sometimes you keep catching fish on squats when bites dry up on bread punch.

Tiny terrors: squats will keep fish grubbing about for ages, without filling them up.

Casters

Maggots might be ideal for getting plenty of bites on the canal, but when you want to single out a bigger stamp of fish, casters are often the answer. These are the chrysalis stage of the maggot, and the bait countless canal experts count on to tempt real net fillers of many species –but especially big roach.

Harvesting your own casters is a time-consuming operation, achieved by continuously separating those maggots which have 'turned', using a riddle which the maggots crawl through, leaving just the inert casters. A much easier solution is to buy casters direct from your local tackle shop.

Casters have an uncanny knack of picking off the quality fish.

However you get hold of them, casters must be stored in airtight condition, to prevent them darkening to the point where they float and become of little use. The easiest way to do this is in a watertight plastic bag. Should you need to keep them for anything over 48 hours, they need to be aired periodically before resealing. On the bank you should cover them in water to keep them fresh and prevent them from turning into dark floaters.

Whether it is their lack of wriggle or dark appearance, casters seem to appeal less to the tiddlers while holding the attention of any bigger fish in the vicinity. They can be fished singly, or in pairs or cocktail baits, usually on hook sizes 14-20. If the fish are really canny, two other dodges are worth a look: darker casters will counterbalance the weight of your hook for a supremely natural presentation, while a size 18 or smaller pattern can be buried inside a caster to fool the canniest of fish.

Worms

Another year-round bait, worms will catch just about every type of canal fish. Many who target perch, bream, tench or eels would feel lost without them in. They

TOP OF THE CHOPS

Not one for the squeamish, the 'chopped worm' technique of slicing up worms to draw and hold fish in your swim is absolute dynamite on canals. Dendrobaenas are perfect for this method, and the classic way is to kick off a swim with several butchered worms and a few casters. The worms can be minced into tiny pieces for a long lasting trail of bloody juices, but generally I also like to leave a few larger worm sections that nuisance fish can't handle.

A pole cup is perfect for depositing 'chop' with total accuracy. Throwing is less reliable over any distance – unless you mix up a little sticky groundbait to bind things together. After an initial, grisly helping you should top up according to bites – usually with another smaller helping of 'choppie' after every decent fish or two. This method is a great way to draw good-sized fish from cover and can be absolutely magical for perch or tench fishing.

Two pieces of broken worm, hooked through the bloody end.

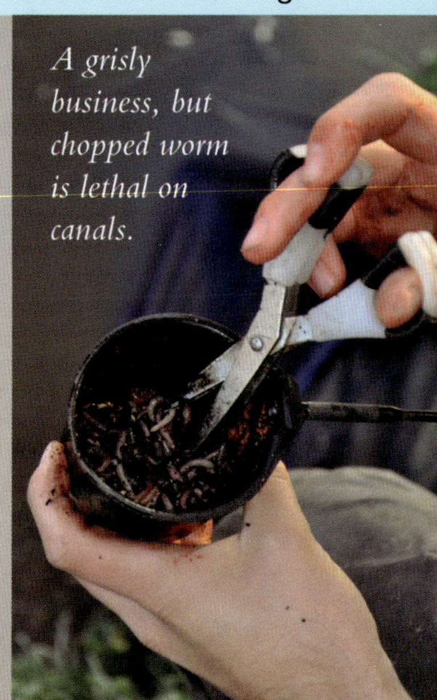

A grisly business, but chopped worm is lethal on canals.

work in the most unpromising of conditions, whether that means icy temperatures or heavily coloured water. Although commercially available nowadays, they also appeal to thrifty anglers who know where to collect them for free.

Lobworms are the largest common species. A wet night on the lawn or local park is the time to gather a supply with a torch in hand. Look closely and you'll spot heads and tails glistening in the damp grass. They can escape rapidly, but if you quickly grab one end, they can be eased steadily out of the ground. Stored in damp moss they will last several weeks. Lobs are rather big for many canal fishing uses but they do deter tiddlers and can be terrific for perch, tench and other species.

Dendrobaenas are perfect size for canal fishing, and easily obtained from compost heaps. Smaller than lobs, they are typically two to four inches long and a reddish colour, sometimes with yellow patches. Whether you use just a nipped off head or tail on a size 18, or a whole worm on a size 10 hook, they are an excellent bait.

Redworms are smaller again, and also found on the family compost heap. These can be used in similar fashion on finer tackle and are great for roach, perch and bream.

Bread

Another staple bait for all canals, bread is cheap and highly versatile. Just about every Cut has locations where locals feed the ducks, and these can have a magnetic attraction for roach and bream. That said, bread will work anywhere you find silver fish. It works throughout the year, but really comes into its own in the winter, when bread is highly visible in cold, clear water. The Christmas match on my local Cut is won virtually every year with bread.

Bread punches form a tidy hookbait, the best have metal heads (detail below).

Bread can be used in various forms, but sometimes the classic big pinch of flake and mashed bread feed are overkill on canals. A more refined way responsible for countless match wins is to use finely liquidised bread as feed and a piece of punched bread on the hook. This is artful, enjoyable fishing, and as well as roach, it produces bream. A fine-tipped float and slow sinking bait are perfect, but perhaps the real skill is in feeding the swim correctly. A walnut sized ball of 'lickie' is ample to start off with, before judiciously topping up with a ball of feed every few fish which is typically little bigger than a twenty pence piece.

It pays to bring different bait options. I caught plenty of fish with bread punch on this occasion, while also feeding chopped worm to a tree for the two chunky perch.

Liquidised Bread and Punch Preparation

Done correctly, liquidised bread is a superb way to draw in fish. Even a small ball of the stuff will explode into a cloud of thousands of tiny, attractive particles that hold the interest of nearby fish.
Here's how it's done:

- Take a white sliced loaf and remove the crusts with a sharp knife. Do remember to keep a couple of slices aside for hook bait!
- Feed 2-3 slices at a time into a food processor, using the finest setting.
- Pass the lot through a riddle to remove any lumps.
- For extra fine crumb, you can freeze and blast the mix again. Otherwise, store in an airtight container.
- Wetted with just a sprinkling of water, this mixture is easily formed into small balls that can be thrown or, better still, deposited using a pole cup.
- Now for the hookbait: take your saved slices and microwave for 15 seconds.
- Now press with a rolling pin.

Voila! You have tacky bread that will stay on the hook beautifully.

For your hookbait, the best solution is to invest in a set of special bread punches – which are tools that cut a perfect little disc of bread for the hook by pressing down on the slice over a hard surface. The hook is then carefully passed through so that plenty of point is showing. Winter anglers will go as small as a 2mm punch on a size 22 hook. Quite often though, a bigger fish or two will also crash the party – so it's worth trying a bigger piece whenever you sense there are better fish in the area.

Hemp Seed

Hemp is another bait synonymous with catching quality canal fish. It can be fed in healthy quantities to keep fish like tench and carp grazing in your swim. More commonly however, it is used to catch roach and has an uncanny knack of winkling out the big ones.

You can buy hemp ready-prepared but it isn't difficult to prepare your own cheaply, and you can also freeze a good supply in small batches. Simply soak it overnight in a large saucepan (avoid your partner's favourite!) before bringing to the boil. Now reduce the heat, cover and let simmer for an hour. You'll know it's ready when the seeds are all opened and the white kernels are visible.

Hemp can be tricky to hook, but is well worth the effort. The easiest way is to find the blunt end and pierce with a sharp baiting needle to make a little hole. Thread a small hook through this and you're away (*see picture below left*). Tares can also be used however, which are much easier to hook and work well in conjunction with hemp. Or you could take a leaf out of a much older book and try elderberries.

Hemp is a terrific roach bait. Piercing one end with a baiting needle makes it very much easier to hook.

Boost your hemp!

Hemp seed is potent stuff straight out of the pan, but can be further enhanced with additives. A small amount of liquid flavouring can be added towards the end of the cooking process, but perhaps the simplest additive is a little salt during cooking. As with all additives, a little added kick is better than overkill.

Elderberries

An old-fashioned bait they might be, but for those in the know elderberries can be devastatingly good for roach and silver bream. They are free too, and you might even find these growing on the canal bank itself. Look out for the reddish-coloured branches and clusters of small, black fruit. They are perfectly ripe in the autumn, when I like to fish them with hemp. A juicy berry slipped onto a size

16-18 hook can be a lovely way to pick off the best roach in the swim.

Groundbait

A huge array of dry groundbaits exist for fishing. While not essential, a decent mix works on several levels. It clouds the water, both attracting fish and giving them the confidence to settle just where you want them. The critical factor is how much and what type you use, because you can easily overdo it.

Aromatic, continental-style groundbaits are ideal for general canal fishing, and lighter types are preferable to heavier fishmeal and 'method' mixes. These can be costly, but by mixing with cheaper brown crumb, a little goes a long way.

Continental groundbaits are perfect for canal fishing.

Mixing Groundbait

- Take your dry ingredients and mix thoroughly in a round-bottomed container.
- Take a separate container of water and add any additives and flavours to this.
- Add the water a little at a time, mixing it thoroughly with the dry powder between the palms of your hands to produce an even consistency. Leave this to stand for a few minutes.
- Once the mix has settled, add a little more water and keep mixing. Try to keep the groundbait light and even textured.
- To improve the consistency and avoid bigger lumps, you might now want to pass the mixture through a riddle. Done correctly, it should squeeze into balls easily, but disperse well in the water without forming a sticky mass.
- You can now add a few samples of bait. It's best to add just a few samples at a time. Go easy on baits like maggots, which can make it tricky to form solid balls of the stuff.

Your groundbait is now ready. A light mix with just a few bait samples is perfect. Unless you're confident the swim is packed with fish, the safest way to start the session is by putting in just a couple of golf-ball sized helpings of groundbait; you can always add more periodically as you get bites.

Ground baiting is an art form in its own right, however. Dark groundbaits tend to give the fish confidence in clear water, with brighter and lighter mixes better in coloured water. The perfect mix is the one that suits your own style of fishing and your local canal, but here are a few suggestions:

Light and Fine: A well-riddled, dark groundbait gives off a lovely cloud that will occupy the fish without giving them too much to eat. For quiver tip fishing, a dryish mix will explode attractively from the feeder.

Sticky: A heavier mix also has its uses for canal fishing. This can be achieved by adding a little extra water, or adding 'binder' to your dry ingredients. This will produce a mix that holds together a little longer – ideal for deep canals and holding larger bait samples such as chopped worm pieces.

Slop: For fishing 'on the drop' you can also mix groundbait extra wet. A nugget of 'slop' at regular intervals will disperse on impact, bringing fish up in the water to investigate; spot-on for summer fishing for roach and rudd.

Sweet Corn

Another cheap, readily available bait, sweet corn is not something that works in all situations, but can certainly be useful for canal tench, bream and carp. Because corn is too large for tiny fish to handle, it makes a more selective bait. It is also highly visible, making it handy for stalking fish in clear water – and the juice from tinned corn is a good additive to give your groundbait an extra kick. Sweet corn should be nicked lightly on the hook to make sure the point shows clearly. Single grains can be presented on a size 16, but two or three grains on a larger hook can be even more effective.

Pellets and Boilies

Although processed baits will never take the place of traditional offerings on canals, they do have their uses. They also have the advantage of easy, convenient storage. High in protein and attractants, they have an appeal to various species.

It is on venues where you find a good mix of stocked fish complementing the natives that off-the-shelf baits truly

You won't get a bite every cast with boilies, but they are pretty much tiddler-proof until a bigger fish arrives – like this tench.

Pellets and boilies: modern baits do have their role, but should be used wisely.

prove their worth. Fish like crucians, skimmers and tench can respond well to smaller pellets, both as feed and on the hook. Use with caution however, because the quantities required will seldom be anywhere near those you might introduce on a heavily-stocked pond. Dampening them lightly before use tends to make them sink better and leak flavour more quickly.

Pellet bands are one way to use the hard variety on the hook, but an easier option is to buy a tub of special, soft, hookable pellets that have a nice rubbery consistency.

Boilies come into their own for carp fishing, although you have two main obstacles to success on this score. Wild fish might need to be familiarised with your chosen hookbait, which is where pre-baiting comes in. Equally, you might find that the bream and tench on your local Cut also take a keen interest in boilies. One answer here is to use really large baits, up to and over 20mm, which only a bigger mouth can handle. That said, 8mm or 10mm boilies are great for chub and other species. Specific flavours are relatively unimportant, but I tend to stick to sweet versions such as tutti-frutti or pineapple for carp, for the simple reason that eels and crayfish love fishmeal-based boilies.

Also worth a quick mention are pastes. These can be bought in little tubs or made at home, usually with fishmeal-based groundbait and a raw egg. On waters that respond well to pellets, a piece moulded round a decent-sized hook can be a good bait, especially in heavily coloured canals.

A bait waiter is an excellent way to keep supplies close to hand, encouraging you to feed regularly.

Particles

Less fashionable but well worth a mention, various particle baits certainly merit a trial for catching carp and tench on canals. The list is endless, but one or two really stand out. Maize and various beans can be good for tench, but my all-time favourite carp bait for canals is the tiger nut. These are ultra-durable and highly selective, with the big advantage that bream don't seem especially partial to them. Which-ever particle bait you try, they must be properly prepared to be safe for fish, usually by soaking and boiling.

Dead and Live Baits

Predatory fish demand a very different menu to the other species. Coarse fish such as roach, bleak and perch can be used live or dead. However, do always harvest your baits from the water you're fishing. Transporting fish between waters is totally irresponsible, not to mention illegal, due to the risk of transferring diseases and parasites. Methods and typical bait sizes are dealt with in the species chapters on the various predators.

A selection of deadbaits for pike. The dyed versions stand out better in murkier waters.

A more convenient and deadly way to catch pike is with frozen sea baits. Here you're spoilt for choice: mackerel, herrings, sprats and a host of others all work. Sardines would be perhaps my first choice for pike, owing to their high oiliness and the fact that they are so soft, your hooks will pull straight out of the bait and into the pike when you strike.

You might catch plenty of pike with plain baits sitting on the bottom, but dyed and popped-up baits can be even more successful. Yellow and red coloured deadbaits stand out well in coloured waters. Lifting your bait off the bottom is another excellent strategy for legering techniques, achieved with the addition of foam or balsa. An even easier solution with whole baits is to carefully inject them with air.

A less popular strategy is to ground-bait for pike, but a simple mix of brown crumb laced with fish oil and chopped pieces of bait is a great way to attract predators, especially in wet, coloured conditions. A suitably bloody mix can be thrown in around your rig, or used in a swimfeeder.

Bloodworm and Joker

Although only used by a tiny minority of specialists these days, these natural baits were once regarded as the most reliable way to put together a good catch on a tricky canal. Bloodworms were seen as so deadly that they were banned on many

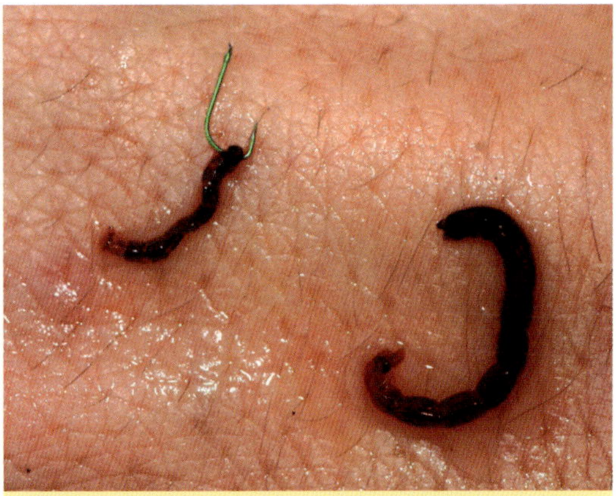

Bloodworms are quite a specialised bait but unbeatable in tough conditions.

waters. Where permitted however, they still make a fantastically natural and effective bait. Every canal contains countless bloodworms in the mud and silt on the bottom, hence even the most wary fish take them without the least suspicion.

In brief, bloodworm tend to be fished on light lines and tiny hooks into the 20s. Jokers are the smaller larvae, which are mixed with damp leam and sometimes groundbait to form balls and used to prime the swim. The method is primarily one which will interest winter match anglers.

POLE CUPS AND CATAPULTS

Introducing bait or 'feeding' the swim correctly is an essential part of canal fishing. While it is sometimes possible to throw small handfuls of bait or balls of groundbait in, this is not always accurate or practical.

Most canal fishing is about short-range accuracy with smallish amounts of bait, hence the ideal canal catapult is not a heavy duty lasher but a smaller model with fine elastic and a cute pouch which, with practice, can deliver regular helpings of bait in a tight area.

When it comes to the ultimate in precision, however, nothing beats the pole cup. Some smaller models can be readily attached and detached from tip sections and used to deposit bait with a rig attached. Most serious pole anglers will have a special, purpose-made 'cupping kit' that will deliver a decent sized ball of groundbait or payload of bait.

Delivering your cargo smoothly takes a steady motion and a little practice. The easiest way, provided you are careful, is to assemble all the pole sections required before adding bait to the cup and attaching the top two. It is then a smooth, passing between the hands before the cup is upended – all achieved as accurately as if you'd fed by hand.

An area is primed for tench. Accurate loose feeding is a valuable skill for the canal-fisher.

ROACH

There is scarcely a canal in the entire United Kingdom that doesn't contain roach. A common fish in terms of distribution, you might say, but certainly not in appearance. From the clearer, rustic canals especially, *rutilus rutilus* can be resplendent with bluish silver scales and vivid red fins. But even a grubby-looking concrete venue can produce fat, flawless roach.

Perhaps no other fish epitomises canal fishing like this species, which for decades formed the staple diet of anglers on the Cut. For many of us, they bring forth nostalgic feelings. Rapid taps on the float tip; my Dad cursing as another bite is missed; the bright gleam of a hooked fish coming to the surface and even that unmistakable smell they leave on your hands. These are the sensations of the roach angler.

Catching a netful of roach was, and still is, an art form on fine tackle. A delicate waggler rig is one way to catch them, but for many canal anglers, roach fishing begins and ends with the unrivalled control and sensitivity of pole and whip fishing.

On many canals you will find roach distributed throughout. Typical shoal fish may average only an ounce but provide bites right through the year. Perhaps the real challenge lies in tempting those larger, broad sided fish that prove a wilier quarry altogether. A fish of a pound or more represents a fine catch, but is always a distinct possibility from any towpath in the land.

Getting the Drop on Roach

The diet and habits of roach vary greatly: they feed on anything and everything from midge larvae to left-over bread missed by local ducks. They can be caught close to the surface or hard on the bottom. The better fish do tend to sit lower in the water than their smaller brethren, but the successful roach angler must be flexible in approach.

The list of baits and methods that catch roach is a long one, but the key to all successful roach fishing is feeding

Depth Tip

Always plumb the depth with great care for roach. A good starting point is a bait just about touching the bottom – but there is a world of difference between 'about right' and absolutely spot-on.

the swim intelligently. Little and often is the golden rule if you hope to keep the interest of a shoal. In the warmer months especially, an enjoyable way to fish is to build the swim in this fashion.

A balanced rig which gives a slow, even fall of the bait will catch roach both 'on the drop' as well as nearer the deck. If you want quantity, a steady stream of maggots or pinkies and possibly some groundbait is a good way to proceed. But how do you pick off the better samples?

Match anglers often get the best of both worlds by fishing two or more different areas (or 'lines') in the swim. The better fish may eventually arrive along with the smaller samples on maggots, but a more certain method is to feed judiciously with more selective baits. The appearance of real 'dog roach', to refer to these giants by their less than glamorous nickname, are fish to savour on light tackle, or transform your fortunes should you be fishing a match.

Liquidised bread explodes into tiny particles on impact – a fantastic way to attract roach in clear water.

Seasons in Silver

The months from summer to autumn are perhaps the most enjoyable of all to fish for roach. Hempseed and casters are both superb baits to pick out a good stamp of fish and the seed comes into its own from May onwards. This is a game of discipline, however. Feed too often and the fish will come up in the water, or charge around giving rapid, easily-missed bites. Instead, introduce ten or so hemp grains or casters every three or four minutes, and those quality roach will eventually settle. I say eventually, because it is wisest to allow at

Above: Double caster. Right: A larger 'dog' roach is a fi make any canal angler happy.

Fine tackle pays dividends when catching canny roach.

least an hour for the fish to feed in peace before you try your hookbait – to the point where they are well-accustomed to mopping up the free offerings undisturbed. The same is true of casters. Feed like clockwork, get the fish settled and those rapid bites will transform into steady deliberate pulls and the chance of Zen-like roach fishing.

Whichever time of year you fish, roach detest crude tackle: opt for the finest-tipped float that conditions will allow, along with fine hooklengths (typically 1½-2lb breaking strain and no greater than 3lb).

The pole is an excellent method, but light running line tactics can also score. On occasions when the water is painfully clear and the roach easily spooked by a pole passing over their heads, the waggler comes into its own. A particularly enjoyable way to catch on the waggler is using maggots or casters, feeding regular small amounts and fishing a slow sinking bait. Roach can be caught at all levels and it's worth trying with the bait set at mid-depth, as well as nearer the bottom. Warm days are perfect for this style of fishing, which suits a busy angler. Indeed, the best roach catchers are restless experimenters, altering the amount and frequency of feed, tinkering with rigs and depths to keep the bites coming.

Dominic's Tip

For winter fishing, sensitivity is crucially important to spot roach bites. Wire-bristled floats are tricky to use, but offer incredible finesse. With these and any other ultra-fine tipped floats, a good dodge is to shot the float so it just about sinks, before greasing the very tip with mucilin or a similar floatant.

Changes of Style

In a certain sense you have a straight choice when roach fishing: do I catch as many fish as possible, or try for fewer but larger samples? The match-style of angling is great for catching numbers of fish, but other methods are both sporting alternatives and better suited to picking out the biggest roach.

There are undoubtedly many more big roach on the canals than many would believe. Perhaps it's simply no longer as fashionable to fish for them. But for the determined roach fanatic, canals can turn up some real surprises. Virtually any canal will produce pound plus roach, which are delightful to catch. But quite a few others have produced two-pounders in the past.

If you're determined to single out a good roach, tackle can be stepped up. A larger bait such as a whole red worm or thumbnail-sized piece of bread flake offers a better degree of selectivity, while the competition angler's favourites such as hemp and casters can still be used to prime an area. Should you wish to avoid the numerous small fish the match crowd want to catch, however, you might be better off introducing bait in larger but less frequent helpings with the aim of settling bigger roach on the bottom. If there are hordes of one ounce fish present, there is also a case for avoiding crumb-based groundbait to cloud the water, which can draw even more of them in.

I have spoken already of the great variety of canal swims and methods, but there are other scenarios where tactics are even more similar to those found on rivers. Several terrific roach spots I know are those near lock gates or inflows where the water is anything but still. These well-oxygenated spots are loved by roach. Besides the usual pole tackle, a stick float would not go amiss, and the same goes for canals that are subject to a steady tow, such as river navigations. If there are bigger roach in attendance, the usual finely-liquidised feed and punch can be replaced by mashed bread and a good-sized pinch of flake on the hook.

In clearer water, such roach fishing demands a cute, natural presentation. In fact the bigger roach can be very fussy when it comes to refusing baits and this is never truer than when the canal begins to tow. A long rod and stick float combination is one effective option, giving superior presentation to a waggler. Perhaps the easiest way to present a perfectly stable bait is to leger, however, and I've had some excellent results with a short, wand-style feeder rod and small swimfeeder packed with mashed bread.

It's uncanny how often the biggest roach of the day arrives late, just as the light drops.

Hemp requires a very disciplined approach but can lead to zen-like roach fishing!

Variety is indeed the spice of life when it comes to canal roach. A less orthodox but delightful way to tempt the species is with an artificial fly, which comes into its own on hot days when fish can be spotted in the surface layers. The little rise forms which dot canals on any given evening are often those made by roach feeding on hatching insects. A light flyfishing outfit is an elegant way to do battle and test the reflexes, and any small dark fly is likely to be accepted. A size 16 or smaller Black Gnat or emerger buzzer is ideal, although wet flies such the Black Spider and Hare's Ear can be deadlier still. Don't retrieve the fly vigorously, but simply let it gently settle, keeping the line taut and striking at any sudden pull or rise. It is not just the smaller roach which will take a fly either, and one of my best ever canal roach of 1lb 9oz fell to a slow sinking wet fly.

Big roach tip

The better roach often hug the edges of the shoal. Try positioning your bait just off your main feed area, or where a few samples have been falling a little further out than the rest.

Year-round Sport

The keen roach angler will certainly not be short on variety in the fishing year. As the days shorten and winter approaches, tactics change again. Hooks and hooklengths get finer (right down to 0.6mm/1lb), bait choices alter and the fish are no longer as evenly spread, having a tendency to congregate in deeper areas. Places with depth and cover such as sheltered bends and marinas are likely areas, as are wider sections. Urban stretches of canal, where the water is slightly warmer and better sheltered also draw concentrations of roach. If you're fishing a match, you must grin and bear the swim you've drawn, but for the pleasure angler, a move is always sensible should you find your starting peg devoid of life.

Winter roach still respond well to regular feed, but your efforts should be more cautious. The fish must be coaxed to feed now, rather than showered with free food. Smaller maggots, by which I mean pinkies and tiny squats, are an ideal way to introduce plenty of free samples without overfeeding the swim. Fine, dark ground-baits are also useful, and these should be riddled and used sparingly. In fact some clear water anglers swear the dark cloud created by a fine groundbait helps the fish to settle.

Ray Minty fed little and often for this net of fish from the Monmouth and Brecon Canal.

Perhaps the best winter roach bait of all, however, is punched bread, which works exceptionally well in clear water. Finely liquidised bread is used as feed, while a small piece of punch goes on the hook. Many winter match anglers wouldn't fish without it. Nor is this just a method for tiddlers. Plenty of winter contests have been won by a run of quality fish taken on bread.

In days gone by, bloodworm and jokers were the method of choice for match fishing, with hooks down to an astonishing size 26. Their use might be limited to match specialists today, but there is still probably no better bait when the going gets really tough.

The art of catching in the cold is to keep the shoal interested without resorting to overkill. The skill is to follow the response of the fish, adding a little more bait when the bites are regular, or backing off when things dry up. It's also worth rotating different areas in the same swim; and trickling casters towards the far bank is worth a try even in icy conditions.

Dominic's Tip

More big roach would undoubtedly be caught on canals if anglers altered their clocks. The tendency for the biggest to show up into evening, just as the light is dipping, is uncanny – it's as if the giants suddenly drop their guard.

Winter roach fishing on the Leeds and Liverpool Canal.

This chunky fish of 1lb 12oz took a good pinch of bread flake.

Taking a good catch of roach on any canal remains a delicate, skilful process. No single gimmick or trick will render you a master – the magic is in putting together of a series of skills. Cute presentation and accurate feeding are constant requisites, as is the prompt, steady guiding away of a hooked fish to avoid spooking its shoal-mates. If carp or pike fishing are a matter of pounds and feet, roach angling is about ounces and inches. The devil is very much in the detail, and anyone able consistently to catch a fine stamp of these pretty fish from canals can consider themselves an accomplished angler.

For sheer numbers, fishing the whip takes some beating.

Russ Hilton took this fine bag on the Grand Union Canal, using a pole cup to lay down a bed of groundbait and fishing maggots and casters over the top.

BREAM

Another almost universal species on man-made waters everywhere, bream are a timeless favourite of the canal angler. For the weekend visitor glued to a float or quiver tip, a bream is so often the best fish of the day to grace the landing net; for match anglers, their presence offers the chance to build a winning weight.

In some quarters these fish are currently rather taken for granted, even maligned. Bream are slimy and docile looking, admittedly. Nor do they fight especially hard, and in fact that bronze, lumbering frame and dozy eye only add to the impression that they live their entire lives in slow motion.

Populations of bream can vary immensely, from small pods of large fish to shoals numbering dozens. Smaller bream which have yet to turn fully bronze (commonly known as 'skimmers') also proliferate on many waters and provide excellent sport. And while Britain's canal networks rarely provide huge individual fish, double figure 'slabs' have been caught on several waterways such as the Lee Navigation and Exeter Canal.

Lessons in Bream

My first infatuation with canal bream began on a wide lock pool. The sight of rolling backs on summer evenings had my brother and I transfixed. The first lesson was simple: you wouldn't get a bite unless you were in the deep, central track of water. Either the fish were very savvy or our tackle was too crude at the time, because they gave only the most gentle of plucks on a quiver tip. We caught so many eels trying for them that a switch to corn was made. It took us a long time to land one and I can still remember the disappointment after the first was hooked and lost, a huge-looking fish that wallowed at the surface before slipping free, agonisingly close to the net.

These wily monsters were probably several years older than my tender age at the time, and provided a tough schooling in the art of bream fishing on the Cut. Looking back on the episode, a few lessons emerge. Bream will sometimes graze over long distances on canals, but there are always key areas that seem to produce fish time and again. Shallows margins are a waste of time, but if you can find any wide, deep areas you will almost certainly find bream. Boatyards and turning bays are capital.

On fairly uniform stretches of water, your best bet is in the deepest water, either at the bottom of the slope each side, or slap bang in the central 'track'. If in any doubt, take a walk on a mild evening in likely areas and you're more than likely to see fish roll. Why they do this is a mystery, but along with bubbles or churned-up silt, those turning backs mean feeding fish.

As dopey as bream look, they can be tricky feeders. This is especially true where fishing is popular, and they are no suckers for crude presentation. Because bream fight only moderately for their size, it is safe to use relatively fine tackle and with balanced tackle, low diameter hooklengths of 2-3lbs are generally adequate. Perhaps the bigger risk is that you'll often find tench and other bonus fish in similar areas.

Balanced tackle should indeed be the watchword for bream fishing, because not only will light tackle provide better fight from this sleepy customer, but forgiving tackle also prevents hook pulls, and the smaller skimmers, especially, have quite soft mouths.

As a confirmed bottom-feeder, bream are one of those species that demand a still hookbait, right on the bed. For this reason, as well as their sometimes finicky bites, the pole represents unbeatable stability and sensitivity. But a feeder

TO STRIKE OR NOT TO STRIKE?

Bream can be tentative biters on the quiver tip. When should you strike? If you're expecting skimmers and the odd bigger fish, any positive movement where the tip plucks and holds should be hit. If tiny bites don't seem to develop, try taking just a little tension out of the quiver tip to see if the fish bite better with a fraction less resistance. The rules can change with a shoal of real dinner plate 'slabs' however. These can give false 'line bites' where the tip pulls rapidly once before bouncing flat, hence it may be best to wait for the tip to pull right round.

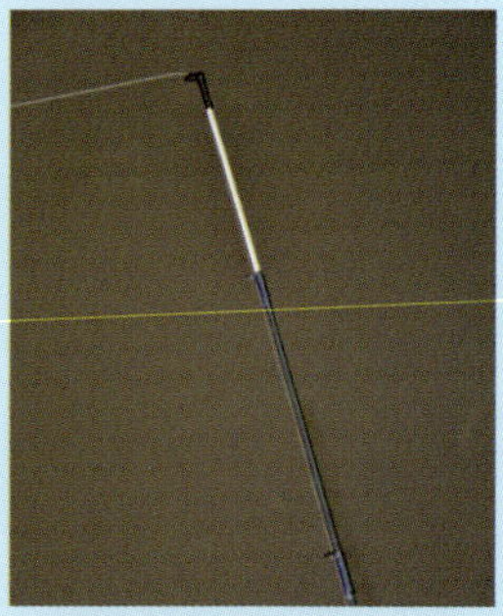

This dark and ancient-looking specimen of over six pounds came right down the central boat track.

rod can quickly become first option on wide sections of canal where a pole won't reach or the weather turns nasty.

Early morning on the Exeter Canal and the author studies a wide bend for signs of rolling fish.

Deads are deadly

Dead maggots are an excellent bait for bream. These are less attractive to small fish and won't bury into the bottom, providing your chosen quarry with an easy mouthful. One quick way to create dead maggots for the hook is to roll them on your knee (as shown). Where real net fillers are expected, try a trio of dead reds on a size 12 hook.

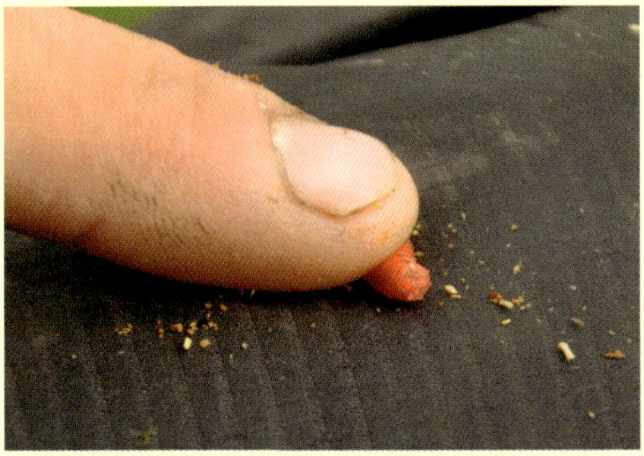

A trio of summer bream cruise in plain sight. In such conditions an early or late session might be best.

Where bigger bream are present, a worm and caster cocktail is a winner.

Maggots catch bream year round, but try a bunch if small fish prove a nuisance.

On wide, open sections of canal, the feeder is a useful bream weapon.

Baiting Strategies

Bream can be taken on all manner of baits. Maggots, bread, corn, boilies – you name it, bream will eat it. Few match anglers would be without worm and casters for bream fishing, however, which are superbly effective. Maggots, including the smaller pinkies and squats, can also work but tend to be less selective. That said, dead maggots are an absolutely first-rate bream bait.

Of course, your hookbait is only the final part of the puzzle for bream. Groundbait is often the key to both drawing fish into the swim and keeping them there, and whether skimmers or large 'slabs' are the target, the species has a particular liking for a potent mix.

The difference a savvy feeding approach makes can be absolutely critical to success. Even an average shoal of fish can eat a lot of bait, so an initial bed of crumb laced with hookbait samples makes perfect sense. This might mean two or three small balls just to test the swim on a tough canal or match conditions, but could also mean a much heavier bombardment where a good net is expected. Your aim is to get the fish feeding vigorously and the advantage of groundbait is that it offers a lot of smell and tiny grains of food to keep a shoal occupied.

Two other useful options are pre-baiting and night fishing. At its simplest, pre-baiting can mean going to a likely spot the evening before your session and introducing a good quantity of bait. This could be several kilos of crumb mix, along with a generous helping of tit-bits: frozen sweet corn or stewed wheat are both cheap and effective.

It's fair to say that early morning and late evening are prime times for bream, but if you seek a really healthy bag of fish it can be well worth staying on into night. On several occasions, years ago, I would head for a canal basin and brave the attentions of night-clubbers and well-oiled pub goers for the chance to plunder a big shoal of bream, which would appear from nowhere as the light departed, demolishing entire tins of sweet corn and anything else you might throw at them.

Alternative Tactics

Most bream anglers might have a favourite formula for success, but the season sees quite a wide variation in approach. Like roach, bream will gravitate towards areas where birds are fed and free food is introduced. I was once pegged near to an old couple's back garden in a winter match and watched with interest as the birds were fed prior to the contest. My neighbour had drawn right opposite the garden and fishing directly over the area with bread, catching several bream and skimmers to build a tidy net.

Bread is an absolutely key winter bait. Tactics can be similar for roach fishing on bread punch, but you can be more liberal with introducing feed and it is well worth trying a bigger hook such as a 12 or 14 with a larger piece of punch.

A proper net-filler from a turning bay, which is always classic bream territory.

The method feeder is a good tactic for bigger bream, turning fussy bites into wrap-rounds.

Out of left field: this three pounder took a wet fly six inches under the surface on a baking hot day.

The disadvantage in winter fishing can be the clearer water, which tends to lead to shoal-mates spooking when you start hooking bream. One solution is to rest the swim, perhaps introducing more feed in a separate area, so you have another line to try should the bream shy off your initial feed.

It goes without saying that bream can respond to swim feeder tactics, but another slightly improbable ploy is the method feeder. This can be absolutely lethal in warm weather, when a frame feeder loaded with sticky groundbait and a very short hooklength can do away entirely with fussy, shy bites and see the fish virtually hook themselves. It might seem crude, but if you can get them feeding hard and cast a method feeder, it's usually a case of ignoring all the taps and simply waiting for the rod to pull right round. Admittedly, a small open-end feeder is better for smaller skimmers, but the method works excellently for the better 'slabs'.

As for the broader habits of bream, these shy fish are a subject of quiet fascination. I have caught the odd fish on lures during May and June, when the fish start to enter spawning mode and can develop a bizarre aggressive streak.

Perhaps my most unusual canal bream captures have been with the fly rod, however. In baking hot conditions, it is not unusual to find a whole shoal of fish simply basking within inches of the surface. They look docile and uninterested, but on occasion I've managed to tempt one of these fish by dropping a slow sinking wet fly into their eye level. Such captures are anything but the norm.

As a final thought, bream fishing often seems at its best during or just after periods of grey, rainy weather. This could be due to the extra colour in the water, levels rising and the canal getting stirred up or simply the species' greater confidence on duller days.

Whatever the theory, grim skies can equal quality bream fishing.

Dull, overcast skies and a wide section of canal – a good combination for bream. Or so Paul Marks was hoping on this occasion.

PERCH

Of all the species that have a knack of thriving on man-made waterways, perch are one of the most universally successful. To my mind they epitomise the attraction of canal fishing. While they are abundant in the most rustic of settings, perch seem to fare just as well in really industrial-looking canals. They respond to a whole range of methods and hold a timeless appeal in the hearts of anglers, from battle-hardened specialists to small children.

The greedy little perch found near any given bridge or access point have formed a starting point for countless canal fishers. In fact my own adventures on the local Cut began with a little gang of us on pushbikes heading for a lock pool. The perch were like us in a sense: bunches of them would hang around in all the obvious places, rather naïve but eager to get stuck in. At the time our tackle was too crude to tempt much else, but along with eels, those perch gave us that vital first taste of success, providing the most obvious of bites and making our cheap fibreglass poles kick.

On other sunny afternoons we would amuse ourselves by throwing bread into the water and watching tiny silver fish swarm over it. Every few minutes a few small perch would arrive to crash the party, launching themselves into the shoal to pick a few off. Another helping of bread and the whole carnival would repeat itself.

The little perch still put a smile on my face, but perhaps the main difference today is an awareness that the next bite could produce a perch of three pounds rather than three ounces. Those great survivors that outgrow and outlast their little siblings do extremely well on canals, foraging on a wide range of prey from fry and gudgeon to crayfish. Nor are they difficult to locate in many cases. Any area of cover and structure, from bridges, walls and lock gates to boats and landing stages can hold them. Equally though, some less obvious places also hold perch and the sloping shelf on each side of the canal is another sanctuary. They do often prefer deeper spots to the shallow margins

Flyfishing is an underrated method for perch

The author tries an urban boatyard.

however, and if you can find relatively deep water slap bang next to snags such as bushes and sunken branches, this is perfect habitat. Failing that, your best bet on more featureless canals is to search the water and pay special attention to any areas rich in small prey fish. At first and last light, which form periods of peak activity, you might even see fingerlings leaping clear of the water as perch go on the offensive.

Footloose Fun

The list of rigs and methods to catch perch is a long one, but the simplest and most enjoyable way to catch them is to rove the banks with lure or fly tackle. In this manner it is possible to try various spots. A light, sporty rod is not only enjoyable to use but minimises lost fish. Perch, and the big ones especially, can be heart-breakers on the wrong tackle; whether it is their head-shaking antics or the soft sides of their mouths, these fish can easily shed hooks, hence heavy rods are less than ideal.

The only risk apart from getting stuck in the odd snag is the presence of pike, which make it sensible policy to use a light wire trace. Braided lines offer terrific strength at a very low diameter – and 10lb braid will cast even tiny lures but minimise the risk of danger should you contact a pike or two.

Des Taylor returns a canal specimen to the haunt it came from, beneath a barge.

Much has been written about lures for perch. While it is perfectly true that a big perch will sometimes take a comparatively huge lure, I am of the firm belief that you will catch a lot more perch on something that can be comfortably engulfed by a pound plus fish in one bite. Lures in the 2-3in bracket are ideal.

There is still something to be said for the classics where lure choice is concerned and a small spoon and plugs, or the time-honoured Mepps spinner still catch plenty of perch. It's good fun just running the spinner through likely areas and watching the fish come after it. One tweak I will often make is to replace the treble hook with a large single: this is much kinder on the mouth of the perch and also allows you to thread half a worm in place, which is a good dodge to earn extra bites.

Of the more modern lures, small soft plastics are brilliant perch catchers. These are much easier to fish at greater depths and hence my first choice when the water is deep or the perch are lying close to the bottom in the colder months. These can be counted down to different depths and retrieved steadily, or even jigged slowly across the bottom. I much prefer those rigged on just a single jig hook, which are also much kinder to the perch compared to treble hooks.

As more anglers cotton on to perch fishing, it's also worth bearing in mind that the species can wise up to pressure. Sometimes it is worth switching to new lures and methods to fool the big, wary fish, whether this means drop-shotting or trying suspending lures or flies which can present an alternative to the ever-popular up and down motion of the soft plastic jig.

INJECTING LOBWORMS

On canals where weed and debris festoon the bottom, a legered worm can be popped up with a little air from a syringe. This must be done with great care on a separate surface because injecting yourself with air can be fatal!

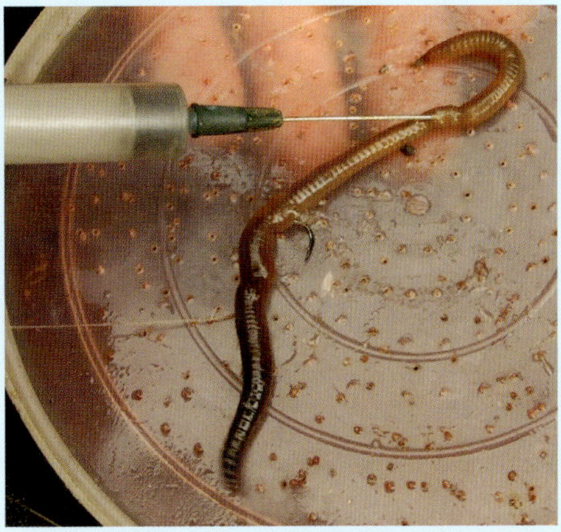

The author cradles a well-marked perch, taken on the worm.

This fish was spotted lurkng menacingly in a clear canal. Note the small fry, seemingly oblivious!

Bait and Wait?

Some things never change in angling. For generations of anglers, perch fishing has begun and ended with a float and a wriggling worm. Our tackle and mindset may have developed beyond recognition but the fish are still suckers for a lively bait, whether this means a delicately pole fished worm section or a whole lobworm. At the most refined end of the spectrum, modern pole-fishing techniques represent an incredibly productive and accurate way to catch perch of all sizes. A pole can be used to sneak a bait into the tightest of corners, while the canny angler can also use the tip to lift and drop a worm enticingly off the bottom.

Some things in fishing never change: perch always love worms.

Typical pole set-ups also offer sensitivity. Slightly thicker-tipped pole floats cater for worm fishing, but otherwise tackle needn't be ultra-heavy. Perch give a gratifying thump but present little danger on balanced tackle: rigs constructed of 3-4lb line and either a light hollow elastic or a solid number eight is ideal for big perch. Some finesse can be a great benefit because although smaller perch can be suicidally eager, the larger fish are surprisingly canny.

Whether it's quality or quantity you want with perch, feeding is crucial. Loose fed maggots are one way to draw in both perch and the prey fish they like to bully. But for the dedicated perch angler there is no better feed than chopped worm. This can be mixed with suitable groundbait and casters, or just pure worm. I find dendrobaenas or red worms best, chopping them into a mixture of fine and larger pieces before they are introduced. I usually kick off proceedings with 6-8 decent-sized worms plus some casters, adding a further 3-4 after every few bites or fish. The effect can be magical, drawing in fish whatever the conditions. A dendroabaena minus head slipped onto a size 12 hook presents an irresistible target amidst a pungent helping of 'choppie', but if smaller fish are a nuisance, lobworms are also worth trying.

Bites are generally very positive, and with the oversized mouth even a small perch possesses, you should strike as soon as the float begins plodding away. For the best in bite-detection and presentation, I like a worm set just touching the bottom.

Seb Nowosiad tries some locks – areas which offer not only cover, but often major depth changes.

Small livebaits also work where they are permitted, but do use a light wire trace as pike insurance.

For anglers who don't pole fish, waggler or light feeder tactics also work for perch. Nor is the classic chopped worm approach the only way to succeed. Maggots are a good bait, albeit one that is not as selective as worm. Like pinkies, they can be very useful to draw in the tiddlers which in turn can switch the perch on. Casters are another option many match anglers swear by for quality perch. I like these as a change bait for later in the session – although they can also be used to tip worm baits.

Going Specialist

For the dedicated specialist angler, selective tactics are perhaps the surest way to target a really big canal perch. The giants are heavily outnumbered by their numerous, mouthy grandchildren and so

for the perch fanatic it can be a case of either wading through the smaller fish or using a large bait.

As with lures, roving tactics guarantee a lot of water is covered. I would recommend just one rod, or at most twin set-ups to cover each side of the canal. A whole legered or float-fished lob worm, sometimes air-injected to sit above weed and debris, is a capital bait for this. As with the match approach, correct feeding can be crucial, whether that means a handful of chopped worm or regularly spraying an area with maggots. Liquidised bread is also excellent: perhaps best of all at drawing in the tiny fish perch love to eat.

Current canal record holder Dan Sales proves it is never too cold to catch perch.

Another option is a small live bait such as a roach or even a small perch. For my part, I dislike this method for several reasons. The presence of pike is one. Light tackle is a bad idea where the species mix. I wouldn't go any lighter than 10lb line and you must also use a wire trace – not ideal, but you'll still catch perch with finer wires. Large single hooks are kinder and less crude than sets of trebles.

Prawns are perhaps the best alternative I can think of to live baits, should you want a really selective offering for perch fishing. These are not often used on canals, but can be very effective at singling out bigger perch.

'Specimen' perch tackle should be qualified as gear that retains some finesse. Hooklengths seldom need be above 5lb strength and it is imperative that rigs are cute and sensitive. Perch are notorious for hating resistance, so when legering, a light bobbin on a long drop is recommended. Perhaps the lightest and best indicator I've ever seen is a simple loop of plastic *(below)* shown to me by Paul Hamilton, the captor of some fantastic canal perch.

The quandary for the specimen perch angler is often the decision whether to stay in one likely spot or search out several, perhaps spending no more than an hour at a time in each promising area. There are pros and cons to both, but in my own fishing, I will only stay put in one swim if I am virtually certain there are good fish present.

Timing can also be crucial. Sometimes you might be in the perfect swim for a big fish but only receive that critical bite early or late in the day. As for seasons, the best time for a real monster is probably in the early spring, before the perch have spawned, although I must stress that big, fat females must be handled and returned with the utmost care. By high summer, weed can make presentation tricky and fish lethargic – and my perching usually only commences again in the autumn. I've found deeper ship canals extremely tough in the winter, but the shallower waters can still produce well in mild, settled conditions.

Further Horizons

Although local rumour can often outstrip the reality with perch, it is my belief that virtually every canal in the country holds the odd two-pounder. A three-pounder is not out of the question, and would be the fish of a lifetime for most canal anglers.

My best fish, a specimen of 3lb 2oz, represents the pinnacle of quarter of a century fishing from the towpath and is a perch I am unlikely ever to better from my local Cut. It was taken on the fly, a less fashionable but utterly deadly way of catching perch where visibility is good. That is another story however. For a far more in-depth look at tricking perch on flies, my book *Flyfishing for Coarse Fish* has a dedicated chapter on special flies and tactics for perch.

Virtually weightless: a simple loop of plastic connected with silicone tubing makes a perfect legering indicator.

TENCH

Another species that exists in surprising numbers throughout canal systems, the tench is a firm favourite with specialists and Sunday anglers alike. They represent a slice of classic British fishing and the inhabitants of our canals can be some of the finest-looking examples you'll ever witness. These fish are a far cry from the pale creatures of commercial fisheries. With deep, velvet-smooth green sides, bright red eyes and broad fins, canal tench are beautiful to behold and tough to tangle with. They do especially well on weedy, clear waters with limited boat traffic, where they take on a delicious, dark-olive complexion.

If it is an enormous tench you seek, canals are perhaps not the obvious place. Typical shoal fish range from 2-3lb, while a 5-pounder should be regarded as an excellent catch. What they lack in weight they often more than make up for in numbers though, with catches of a dozen or more fish possible if you can pin down their whereabouts. To a pleasure angler this represents terrific sport; to a match contestant, the chance of a winning weight of fish. Either way, the angler who catches tench from the local Cut goes home feeling happy.

Left: Tench love to hug cover such as lilies. A pole offers pinpoint presentation.

Why wait till June?

Misty mornings and tench bubbles are all part of fishing folklore and any old textbook will tell you that the time to start is in June, with a float amongst the lilies. This doesn't always ring true with modern canal fishing however and the belief that you won't catch tench early in the year is a false one. Could this be down to the wetter, milder winters that are becoming increasingly normal? Some terrific bags of tench have been taken as early as January in kinder weather, and the fish can often be found in concentrated groups well before

BACKWATER TENCH

It's a curious phenomenon, but tench invariably thrive best on canals with little or no boat traffic. Why should this be true? Whether it is the lack of weed, or difficulties spawning where there are chemicals and disturbance, populations always seem to be less abundant on shallow canals where boats dominate.

Green velvet: with good looks and serious muscle, the appeal of canal tench is obvious.

the magical June 16th. My own cue to start casting for them is the appearance of Dave Sellick's bike on the towpath of Exeter Ship Canal, fairly rattling with tackle. Setting up on a wide, deep section, it is not unusual to see him bent into a solid fish in March, or even February.

On any canal with a good population of tench, the fish seem to favour particular areas over others. An excellent starting point is to ask at your local tackle shop, where staff will know where the most recent catches have been made. Another good resource are match results on the internet; tench often decide the winner at club and open contests and you can quite often track down the exact stretch and even the numbered pegs where fish were caught.

What do tench look for in their choice of habitat? Sheltered, weedy areas are ideal and, yes, lily beds are not just easy on the eye for anglers in this context. Stretches where the canal broadens out are also classic, and even in quite urban surroundings they can quite often be found in the turning bays also favoured by bream.

Should you be in any doubt, an early morning walk is likely to yield further evidence. Trails of tiny bubbles are the classic clue, and if the fish are feeding hard you might see bursts of stirred-up silt.

Aside from the cooler months when you occasionally spot a sleepy fish or two slap bang in the deep central track of small clear canals, the key area for tench is often at the bottom of the sloping shelf on each side of the canal. Where this deepening contour meets a weed bed is even more ideal.

A Newport Canal fish comes to the net.

Good Habits

Although not essential, there are two strategies for tench that could catapult that early morning on the canal from mediocre to mind-blowing: raking and pre-baiting. A weed rake *(see the tackle section)* is a great way to clear a swim for fishing on a neglected canal. Not only does this render tangled areas fishable, it also stirs up the bottom, dislodging food and creating a commotion that is sure to draw the inquisitive tench.

Exeter Angling Centre's Dave Sellick had a real battle with this canal cracker.

Raking can also be combined with pre-baiting, which is simply the act of priming your chosen swim with suitable bait well before you cast out. This can be done the night before, or indeed across several visits in the days leading up to your next trip. Baits needn't be costly for this, and fine particles are ideal to keep the tench occupied for long periods in one area. Parti-mixes offer one solution, but perhaps the all-time classic is a mixture of stewed hempseed and sweet corn.

Whether you've prepared in this fashion or not, tench are definite creatures of habit. They have favourite patrol routes and, equally, favourite times to feed. In warm summer weather, an early start is almost invariably peak time, although late in the day is also good. In the cool climes of early spring, the late afternoon, when the sun has had a few hours to wake the fish up, can be the best period to try.

The weed rake is an excellent way to create your own 'hot spot'.

It has been said repeatedly that tench don't feed at night or in the middle of the day. These are not the best times, but I leave you to draw your own conclusions. I once caught a tench at 3am in March while waiting for the elusive carp on one of my local canals; I had a job bringing it in because my landing net had frozen solid to the bank.

Tinca Tactics

The number of baits that have been successful for tench is lengthy, but there are three offerings I wouldn't leave home without: worms, casters and bread. Maggots can also be excellent, but are liable to draw the attention of nuisance fish, so as many as four or five on a size 10 or 12 hook is often a better option than a small bait.

Tench respond well to feed, but how much you add depends on circumstances. If you are confident that tench are in the vicinity, bombarding the water could spook them, so just a little loose feed is a sensible starting point. If it is likely to be more of a waiting game, laying down some groundbait laced with samples of your hookbait, is a good policy to attract any passing tench and hold their interest. My all-time favourite combination is a potent mix of chopped worm and casters, bound together with a little continental groundbait. A red worm and caster cocktail on the hook would be my first choice; although if the Cut is alive with small fish, sweetcorn or even pellets can be invaluable. Bread is an excellent choice for clear weedy water, as a good pinch will settle gently and not disappear into the bottom.

The specimen fishing scene is awash with leger rigs for tench these days, but for the canal angler, float fishing remains the staple diet. A waggler set-up, or indeed the classic 'lift method' are two ways to proceed. Neither can match the precision of pole fishing though. This is an incredibly accurate way to sneak a bait among lilies or slap bang down the far slope of the canal.

There is little place for delicate tackle with tench. These are fish which can surge hard in the direction of cover and decimate light rigs. They also have fairly poor eyesight. That said, they can be resistance-shy, and this is perhaps one reason that carp-style set-ups are poor in comparison to balanced float tackle, set with sensitivity.

The exception to this rule would be a wide section of canal, or blustery days, when a swimfeeder set-up forms the best option. I like a groundbait feeder packed with the same sort of chopped worm and caster mix I prime my pole fishing swims

With no closed season on most canals, traditional rules don't always apply. Russ Hilton took this thirty pound bag of tench on a cold day in March!

The pole is far and away the most efficient way of catching canal tench.

with. Accuracy is paramount, and just as important as when you're targeting bream.

Line of 4lb should probably be regarded as an absolute minimum strength, even in very open swims. Usually, a low diameter hooklength of 4-5lb breaking strain is sensible, but I would go as high as 6lb straight through in weedy locations. They are not desperately tackle-shy and if you can get the fish feeding hard they won't balk at fairly robust tackle.

The pole fisherman should use a tough elastic where snags exist, and look to guide a hooked fish away from sanctuary immediately. This does not necessarily mean wrenching the pole back, which can cause a hooked tench to fly off in a frenzy. Better to guide the fish away firmly but steadily from danger, and if you can get the tench into the clearer, central channel before he builds a head of steam up, so much the better.

Stick it out or Search?

As with virtually any species on our canals, you can be as patient or as mobile as you like in pursuit of tench. You can try and attract the fish to you; or you can track them down. If you are confident of their whereabouts, the sit and wait approach has its merits. Even if you are not bang on the money, patrolling tench could arrive sooner or later. What does seem clear is that different spots vary greatly for tench. In some areas they seem to settle routinely, perhaps because these places offer the richest feeding; other spots just see the occasional 'passenger' and rarely produce a good bag. The moral is simple: whether through a local tip-off or simple trial and error, seek out those consistent holding areas on your local canal and you will rarely be disappointed.

If you are new to a water, or just have itchy feet, the roving approach is more suitable. With a minimum of tackle and polarising glasses, you are free to roam in search of showing fish and likely spots. On murky canals this is harder work, but you can easily put a little bed of bait into three or four locations and hop between them to see if the fish are there. You may not necessarily see the fish themselves, but trails of little bubbles, swirling tail patterns or patches of disturbed silt are a giveaway. Again, small particles are ideal – two or three good handfuls of hemp, with a few hookbait samples mixed in will keep the tench busy for quite a while.

Where stalking tench gets feverishly exciting is on those quiet, seldom-used canals with abundant weed and clear water. Baits like bread and corn are ideal for shallow venues because you can immediately see if the free bait you've been throwing in has been eaten. In clear water, an offering that stands out against the bottom is ideal and I've even caught tench on artificial flies on a couple of the clearer canals near my home in the West Country. My favourites are large nymphs that are easily spotted and stand out against the bottom. It is fascinating, if sometimes frustrating, sport.

The methods, baits and surroundings are therefore varied for the tench angler. I can't ever remember catching a vast specimen on any canal. The only conclusion this leads me to is the total inadequacy of pounds and ounces to define fishing pleasure, because the hump-backed, strong and richly coloured tench of rural canals are the most beautiful I have ever sunk a net under, bar none.

Trails of small bubbles are the classic giveaway that tench are present.

A beautifully-conditioned mirror and a knackered but very happy angler.

CARP

That Britain's canals contain some huge specimen fish is no longer a secret. Nevertheless, the sheer quantity and quality of untapped carp fishing remains an eye-opening phenomenon. Should this be such a surprise? Stock fish released by angling clubs in past decades are thriving, as are accidental and not-so-accidental escapees. They find rich feeding grounds and plenty of space. And as a hardy, long-lived species, these carp can become fish of spectacular size and beauty.

My interest in canal carping first started on the Exeter Ship Canal. Club records documented commons and mirrors stocked in its waters a little after World War Two. Some fifty years later in the 1990s, these fish had thrived for decades undetected. As a boy I would witness fish that rendered me incapable of rational thought: huge, barrel-shouldered carp with mouths that could swallow your fist. One of these survivors came out at over 40lb, a canal record at the time.

Such circumstances might seem exceptional, but the seeds have already been sown for the next generation of monsters on our canals. Perhaps a majority of Cuts now hold fish to over 20lb. If in any doubt, a customary glance at the reference section should provide all the evidence required. Canals such as the Grand Union have a terrific head of fish, while countless other waters also hold fish from Bude to Glasgow. And yet this is the tip of the iceberg. So much water is unfished and those who are catching big carp rarely share their locations.

With miles of water to roam, canal carp can present challenging fishing. It can be a time-consuming, soul-searching business. You will undoubtedly experience failures as well as successes. In a sense it is the challenge and mystery that is the essence of the exercise. You might have little track record to work with: canal

Tackle up Tough!

Where large carp exist on many canals, the biggest challenge is landing the fish. In the words of Midlands canal fanatic Tony Keeling: 'You'll hook 'em, but that's about as far as you'll get!' These fish are not as tackle shy as those constantly bothered by bivvy anglers on stocked waters however, so why fish light? A sensible minimum would be 15lb line where fish run big, although where permitted, 30lb braid is far stronger and better at cutting through weed.

carpers tend to be secretive. You might have to set up in tight swims well away from the obvious access points. But what a feeling to connect with a solid, beautifully-conditioned fish that might never have been caught before.

There are admittedly other canals where stretches have been flooded with 'match sized' carp too, and I will cover these later in the chapter. Whether this is desirable is open to debate, as carp are greedy fish that can have an adverse effect on both water quality and the other species that share the same habitat. To my mind the perfect model for angling clubs is to trickle stock with fewer fish, giving them plenty of space to grow on without affecting the canal.

A sight to make any carp angler drool: a whole gang of fish loiter in a boatyard.

Carping Clues

While success on some carp waters can be all about smart rigs and clever tactics, canal fishing is refreshingly simple by comparison. The fish seldom see a fraction of the pressure you find on day ticket lakes. Nine times out of ten, the biggest obstacle

SPAWNING SITES

Each year, carp congregate in certain areas to breed and this can see spectacular numbers of fish. Different strains breed at different times too, and these sites can be good places to fish, as rival carp often move in to mop up eggs. Just ask the current canal match record holder Paul Turner, who drew the perfect peg to cash in with over 100lbs of mostly double-figure carp!

Spawning carp are vulnerable, however. Fluctuating weather can see spawn-bound carp die. When spawning sites can be little more than a foot deep, they are also at risk from boats speeding through. Certainly, carp seem to survive longer on deeper canals or waters that are quieter and offer plenty of sanctuary.

to success is finding your quarry in the first place.

The first step is often a walk with polarising glasses. You're looking for any signs of life, whether that means basking fish or areas the fish are likely to settle. I cannot stress how important it is to pick the right area to fish. Nobody gets it right all the time, but you could wait a week without a bite in the wrong swim.

Canal carp have very definite patrol routes. There will be areas they move through and others where they feed, so don't assume that by spotting a couple of fish you've found the best area to set up. Just observe: where are they moving towards? Do the fish pause to feed or investigate, or are they merely travellers? With practice and careful observation you can often tell within a few seconds if any individual carp is catchable or not.

While canal carp can be nomadic, it's also fair to say that they tend to frequent the same areas time and again. Wide areas such as turning bays and boat yards are often a key area. Indeed, boats seem to possess a magnetic attraction for carp. On some canals they are prolific around moored craft and can be seen in plain view, where they become so at home that boat owners feed them like pets. The regular headache for many canal anglers is that these are also 'no fishing' zones.

More 'natural' spots can also be great areas. Carp like the shade and sanctuary offered by tree cover, bushes, reeds and lilies. Bends are another classic spot, as are inflows, outflows and passing points where the canal widens or narrows. In the absence of finding an area where carp settle, you can guarantee that moving fish will pass through these areas.

On many canals you might be the only angler a carp ever sees.

A word of warning. No matter how fishy a spot looks, you can spend a lot of fruitless hours by being inflexible. Far better to try several spots over a period of hours, days and weeks rather than stick it out in one area. On prolific canals, you might try each spot for about an hour at most. Even on the toughest canal, if I have not had a run in two nights in any one location, I would usually try elsewhere.

An increasing number of canals have their local 'hot spots', but the best fishing is not always readily accessible. Perhaps it's a sad indictment of modern carp angling, but if you can find any promising area more than 400 yards from a car park, or without obvious room for a bivvy, it's unlikely anybody is fishing it. Unless you're a lazy angler, this is to your advantage.

In general terms, the long, open canals with big expanses of water can be the most testing for fish location. And perhaps easiest of all are those canals where lock systems present separate, enclosed 'pounds', each with its resident head of carp essentially restricted to one area.

Simple Beginnings

The slightly better news as far as canal carping goes is that you can put your confidence in very simple rigs and presentations. In the warmer months, an excellent way to start fishing is with a free-lined bait in likely areas. Bread and dog biscuits are two cheap, effective offerings and it is simplicity itself to roam the banks with a single rod looking for cruising carp. Even if you see nothing in a good-looking spot,

CRAYFISH TROUBLE!

While there is no perfect solution when it comes to avoiding bream and crayfish, certain steps can definitely help. Trying bigger baits, tough particles and longer hairs on your rigs are ways to make your offering more 'selective'. Tiger nuts, in particular, are an excellent carp bait that both crayfish and bream find harder to deal with. Where crayfish are present in numbers, there is little you can do other than check and recast your bait regularly. Using special bait skins to toughen boilies or even plastic and rubber baits are another option, although even a plastic bait can only withstand so much punishment from the signal crayfish menace!

Shredded bait: the infamous crays strike again!

On ship canals especially, carping can be a waiting game.

it is worth introducing a few biscuits or pieces of floating bread to see if any fish will come up. It is well worth seeing if you can get the carp taking confidently before casting out – and this can be the difference between getting one chance and possibly catching several fish.

On the typical narrow canals, you will easily be able to hit the far bank with a single piece of bread crust. A light specimen or barbel rod is ideal, as are the shorter 'Stalker' style carp rods and I would fish a low diameter 10lb line direct to a size 6-8 hook for this operation. Around boats especially, the fish can be bold takers that require prompt action on the strike to keep them from tangling with snags and obstructions.

Two common problems are ducks and 'no fishing' zones. The latter can be frustrating, but confrontations with boat owners should be avoided at all costs on these shared waters.

One way to deal with the issue is to fish just outside prohibited areas: quite often, with regular loose feeding, it is possible to draw carp into legitimate water. My angling friend Dan Sales is a master at this art, as well as a smooth negotiator when it comes to boat owners!

Ducks and other waterfowl are another common problem, and perhaps this problem is exacerbated by the fact that carp love to frequent areas where ducks are regularly fed. One solution is to take plenty of bait and effectively feed two areas, one for the carp and a separate area to keep water birds well clear of your bait.

Another dodge is to anchor or 'zig rig' a buoyant bait a few inches beneath the surface where the ducks won't find it so easily but your offering is still available to a cruising carp. A good chunk of crust is perfect for this approach, although where hordes of roach demolish bread, a pop-up boilie is usually the answer.

A tight swim on the Grand Union; note the short rods and minimal amount of gear.

Above all, do be vigilant when it comes to birds, boats and people. An amenable, considerate angler is a friend to all but the most bloody-minded of canal users; an unreasonable one sets a poor example for all of us.

Tails Up

Bottom fishing might be the first choice method of many carp anglers, but on the canals legering represents a very different challenge. Boats, bream and crayfish can scupper the most perfectly presented rig, while the average towpath certainly wasn't designed with the typical carp angler in mind.

Some canals do have areas where long-stay angling is possible, but a better starting point is usually to travel light with just one, or at most two, rods. This way the angler can stay mobile and avoid bother with cyclists, boaters and other canal users.

End tackle can be kept extremely simple, such as a straightforward bolt rig set-up. My usual bait preference is for a pop-up boilie, simply because this keeps the bait out of silt and debris and renders it supremely easy for a passing carp to find. The fish are seldom heavily pressured, so a potent smelling, obvious bait such as a bright pop-up is ideal. In many cases, back leads are also essential to keep your main line pinned to the bottom and clear of passing boats, canoes and water birds.

As with fishing floating baits, bottom fishing is all about location. Bottom browsing carp are not as easy to locate as surface cruisers, but do sometimes give themselves away by bubbling, stirring up the bottom or rolling. They particularly love tight spots such as far bank snags, so accurate, underarm casting is the order of the day.

When it comes to feeding, caution should be exercised on canals. Many waters have a good head of bream and the introduction of bait en masse can see your swim invaded by these slimy residents. Hence a safer option is to introduce just a handful of bait and a small pva bag of goodies along with your hookbait; this represents a nice accurate solution.

Pre-baiting is another way to draw in and settle carp in an area, but it must be done with caution. A big bed of small particles such as hemp and maize is certainly harder for bream or crays to obliterate. I combine this with a few large boilies or, better still, big tiger nuts. Introduced every few days in a handful of areas, you are likely to interest resident carp even if nuisance species also take their share.

Match Tactics

With the huge popularity of 'commercial' carping, it's perhaps inevitable that angling clubs seek to stock canals with smaller carp to boost both pleasure and match fishing results. Furthermore, I have no desire to present canal carping as a narrow field: as well as the specimen approach, the species lends itself well to

Taking aim on the towpath.

Carp rigs needn't be fussy. Popped-up baits avoid debris and are easy for carp to inhale.

modern match fishing techniques.

Pole fishing is an excellent way to get amongst hard fighting fish where stock levels are high. Presenting rigs to far bank features is exciting stuff, but should also come with a warning: typical canals are more snaggy and cramped than the average commercial. This aspect, along with the very real prospect of a double figure fish snaffling the bait, calls for tough tackle and strong arm playing. Heavy elastics are ideal, and I much prefer modern hollow types. I would also opt to avoid lighter hook links and go for at least

A battling fish is brought to the net after snatching a pop-up boilie.

6-8lb line fished direct. Strong, smash-proof floats which can be rigged directly through the body are ideal for the job.

Baits for this style of fishing are similar to commercial fisheries. Corn and pellets are a great choice in the warmer months, while worm and casters work year round. A common tactic is to feed fairly generously, but let the fish get their heads down confidently for an hour or two before dropping in for a bite. Carp can crop up anywhere, but will venture into shallower water than the likes of bream wherever you find cover.

On wider sections of canal, other methods also come into play. The waggler can work, but perhaps the deadliest match-style method of all for bays and turning basins is the method feeder. This is certainly true for wider venues such as the Bude Canal near me.

Is carp-hauling from a canal strictly cricket? Traditionalists might shake their heads. But admittedly, it can be a lot of fun and also switch more weekend anglers away from the usual muddy pools and give them a taste of canal fishing.

The Long Game

Perhaps the most challenging but exciting canal carping of all is on those waters where the head of fish is smaller but there are some uncaught giants present. In these circumstances, the 'bait and wait' approach can come into its own. Such has been my own experience on the Exeter Ship Canal where fellow fishing nut Norbert Darby and I spent large chunks of one summer surviving on little more than cider and blind optimism.

At one point the mathematics themselves became quite terrifying: kilos of bait, days of fishing, the occasional bream and just one moment of brief delirium when Norbert's rod went into meltdown and a fish stripped twenty yards of line before smashing up 15lb fluoro-carbon. A few lessons were learned. One was to stick with tiger nuts on this particular water; another was to avoid barbless hooks at all costs in the weed. We also tried using leads attached to weak links, aimed to detach on the strike. This helped prevent carp burying themselves in the weed.

I lost a lot of sleep that summer. Part of it was the fear that I'd be dozing when the key moment arrived; the rats and stranger towpath users might also have had something to do with it. It's certainly good policy to fish in company in any urban areas and also be wary about leaving your car in spots frequented by local oiks.

Perhaps I escaped lightly. One morning Norbert woke up riddled with midge bites from his neck to his nether

Dan Sales displays a mint-condition mirror carp: uncaught fish like this await the determined angler on countless canals.

If you can spot the fish, success can be as simple as a free-lined chunk of bread crust.

regions. Eventually though, after two location changes, we made inroads. And in fact the more we suffered, the more determined we became to put a carp in the net.

The 'hot' time for a take seemed to be just as dawn broke and our moment of truth came one cool morning in July. Having fallen out with his girlfriend at the time, Norbert came down to the canal and slept on the floor of my bivvy with just a coat for a blanket. At around six in the morning I nearly tripped over him as one of my alarms went beserk and something substantial ripped off down the canal. It was a long ten minutes getting that fish in. One moment she was in open water, the next totally bedded in near bank weeds. In my panic, the reel tangled and I had to virtually handline the final few yards, praying that somewhere in the weed was the carp we'd waited so long to catch. The fish went 15lb and was as beautiful as any mirror carp I'd ever caught. In an instant, all the insomnia and midge bites were forgotten.

This is the joy of canal carping. It only takes a single bite for despondency to turn into delight. That heave on the end of the line could be a 10-pounder or a 30-pounder and either way, it's likely to be a beautiful fish you'll never forget.

A hat-trick of chub wrestled from cover on the pole. These splendid fish fell to chopped worm and caster.

CHUB

Although the chub is widely regarded as a classic British river species, their widespread presence on many canals more than merits special attention. Nor are these solid golden-bronze fish a poor relation to those found in running water. To take just one example, I will never forget the day my friend Seb Nowosiad hooked and landed a huge fish on the Kennet and Avon Canal. We had assumed that the thumping presence on the line was a pike, before a fish rolled that left us both speechless. At just an ounce shy of 7lb, this was a monster to open anyone's eyes to the potential of giant chub from Britain's towpaths.

The fact that this beast took a small lure also highlights the diversity of methods that can be used to catch chub. A broad spectrum of approaches is equally valid, from pole fished worms right through to specimen tactics and even artificial flies. In short, whichever method you prefer to use on the local Cut, the chances are you'll be able to target chub if they are present.

Perhaps that should come as little surprise, because chub are incredibly adaptable. It is this versatility and wide-ranging predatory diet that explains their great success on canals. From fly life to roach fry, discarded baits to crayfish, little escapes the keen eyesight and bold mouth of the chub.

Canals that meet with rivers are one explanation of rogue chub populations, but in many other cases their presence is the direct result of stocking programs. Such has been the case on many waters such as the Shropshire Union and Taunton to Bridgwater Canals. Introduced to boost catches, fingerlings of this greedy species don't stay small for long. Nor are these wily survivors short-lived. Fast forward a few years and the resulting beasts weigh pounds rather than ounces. And what phenomenal fish they are: cunning and sometimes easily spooked, yet eminently catchable for any single-minded angler who knows where to look.

Dominic's Tip

They might be spooky fish at times, but chub are also a naturally inquisitive, aggressive species. The angler can capitalise on this by imparting some movement into their offerings. Pole anglers in particular can earn extra bites by regularly lifting and dropping their baited rigs. Chub will often home in and make a grab as the bait is falling or settling in the water.

Chub are lovers of cover and shade. Several were lurking under this barge on a hot day.

Cut Kings

Des Taylor tries close to some lock gates, often a good feature for chub.

Despite being present on many canals, chub are anything but evenly spread. Fish the wrong area and you might never see one, whereas a favourite hideout could be the home of a dozen fat fish.

Like perch, chub can be reassuringly predictable in their haunts and habits. They are lovers of shade and cover first and foremost. Bridges, lock gates, tree cover and moored boats are all likely places to find them. Sometimes it is possible to lure them out with free food, but in general terms chub fishing is about presenting your offering as close to cover as you dare. This is never truer than in less than ideal conditions and as a general rule, the brighter and sunnier the day, the tighter you'll find the local chub clinging to any available shade. I once caught several of over 3lb on a baking hot day, but only by using a pole to lower a worm right under the hull of a barge on the far bank.

Other likely areas are more akin to river fishing lies. Chub certainly like little inflows and can sometimes be found in the streamier water just below lock gates. Baits can be trotted under a decent-sized float in such cases and the fish will often lie just off the main flow of water, where they can happily pick off any passing morsels.

Chub are not the most powerful of fish, but their love of snags combined with a bludgeoning fight render light tackle foolhardy. Line of 4lb should probably be seen as a minimum, but where chub run large and obstacles are present I would have no hesitation in stepping up to 6-8lb strength. Hooks, likewise, need to be strong enough for the job. Whether your choice is a size 16 to present double caster or a size 6 for a lobworm or boilie, I prefer a forged, wide-gape pattern. And while to some extent it's true that you'll earn more bites with finer tackle, there's absolutely no point in hooking a fish you can't land. With chub there is also a strong case for doing away with a weaker hooklength entirely. Indeed, my preference for either running line or pole fishing is to fish "straight through" with no connecting knot that could suddenly part.

Methods and baits can vary a great deal, but will be dictated to some extent by water clarity and conditions. A good general rule is to avoid busier times of day with boats and pedestrians, when resident chub often go into hiding. Many are the times when the fish suddenly switch on as boat and human traffic die down, or bright weather is replaced by cloud cover.

A Varied Approach

The behaviour and appetite of chub is legendary in its variety, so many methods will work. A lot depends on the type of canal and water clarity you find. If the chub can be spotted at close quarters, there is a lot to recommend complete simplicity. Clearer, rural canals are perfect for the free-roving, light tackle approach. A free-lined piece of bread crust or lob worm is about as basic as it gets, but provided you haven't spooked your chub, the reaction can be instant. If you can stalk individual fish, loose feeding or groundbaiting can be rendered unnecessary, or at least only worth trying if a preliminary cast or two doesn't produce. The sudden introduction of handfuls of bait could easily put the fish off, and that big chub might just as likely scoff the first morsel it sees, provided you keep low and cast carefully.

The same is true of artificial flies and the summer months can provide some truly thrilling fishing with basking chub. I've taken them on both wet and dry flies on clear canals, including a fish of 3¾lb that took a small streamer cast under a bridge.

Russ Hilton cradles a 4-pounder from a Midlands canal.

Lure fishing can also produce the goods with sufficient water clarity. I suspect that a lot of the time chub respond to a lure with curiosity or outright aggression, rather than a natural "feeding" response. They will occasionally hit big lures, but if I single-mindedly wanted chub, my lure choices would be small, 2-3in models. Floating or surface popping plugs can be great provokers, and the more vigorous the better. Small spinners and jigs can also work and although lures don't catch huge numbers of chub on canals, they do tend to appeal to the bigger, meaner fish of over 3lb.

It is the more coloured water where bait fishing tactics tend to dominate. This is certainly true on the Midlands canals, where chub loiter amidst stirred-up water and boat traffic. It stands to reason that baits with strong scent come into their own. Nor is coloured water necessarily a drawback: chub find it harder to spot the angler and spook less easily in such environs. Where you might pick off only a single fish in clear water, muddier canals have hotspots where you could catch multiple fish in a day.

Bait fishing approaches for chub could be divided into match and specimen styles, depending on whether your aim is to catch as many fish as possible or single out a real beast. Ground bait is not strictly necessary for chub, but regular helpings of loose feed certainly make sense in coloured water – and it can pay to do this for a good hour or two before you introduce a hookbait.

On clearer canals, flyfishing offers terrific visual excitement.

Pole fishing is the natural choice for many. The pole is ideal for dropping a bait tight to those snaggy lies loved by chub, where the rod and line angler takes their life in their hands. A typical set-up would consist of 4-5lb line straight through, along with a thick bristled float to accommodate baits such as a whole red worm. Elastics must be strong (typically a size 12 or hollow elastic) and not set too loose if you are to win the initial tug-of-war with a hooked chub in the vicinity of obstacles. A prompt response is called for and this can be a thrilling, if hair-raising, experience.

Perhaps the best recipe for chub on the pole is the use of chopped worm and casters. An initial helping of 8-10 dendrobaenas and a few casters, mixed with a little soil or dark groundbait is capital, to be topped up at intervals or after every fish by a smaller amount of bait. A juicy worm, broken in half and presented on a size 12 hook, is an excellent morsel for chub, possessing both scent and wriggle.

Chub will feed at all levels of the water. You might argue that they are happiest in mid-water, but baits fished on the bottom most often catch the biggest fish. Specialist legering tactics certainly have their place, whether you use a bobbin-style indicator or quiver tip

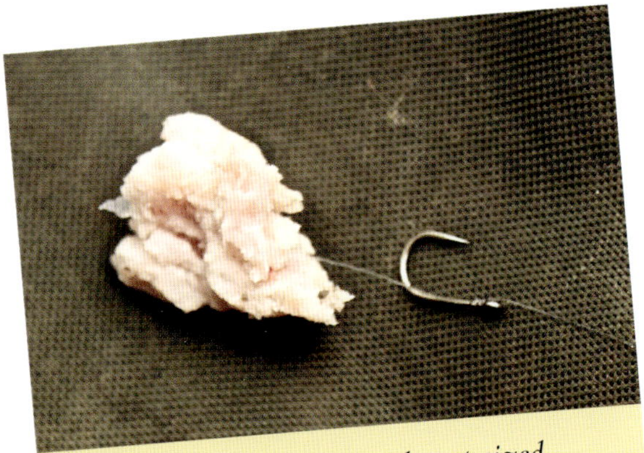

Chub have big mouths: a decent-sized chunk of meat or boilie are a good bet in coloured water.

set-up. As for baits here, a whole lobworm is one option but there is probably no finer choice than a good-sized chunk of luncheon meat or a boilie. I'm certainly not going to argue with Des Taylor, who catches some huge canal chub on specialist tactics. A 20mm boilie or chunk of meat the size of half a matchbox wouldn't be too big. Hair rigging is one way, but many chub specialists prefer side hooked baits, believing they connect with more bites.

It's also true that chub are caught on much smaller baits such as maggots or bread punch, often by a happy accident when anglers target a mixed bag. But if you are determined to catch a chub by design, it does pay to be selective, and where visibility is poor, a good mouthful makes sense.

Perhaps the single most important decision with chub fishing is swim choice. When in doubt as to their whereabouts, the "bait and wait" approach is a gamble. You're much better off travelling a little lighter and trying several likely spots in the course of a session. That said, many canals have "known" chub hot spots. Tackle shops and match results are both good sources of information.

Where exactly the best canal chub fishing in Britain is found is open to debate, but my reference section should provide some useful clues. For sheer beauty and visual sport, the canals of rural Wales take some beating. Then again, for numbers and size of chub, the canals of the Birmingham area are probably unsurpassed. A whole series of short pounds between lock gates exist on the Dudley canals, for example, where you can be confident that the residents are in close proximity. And while any canal chub of 3lb plus should be regarded as a fine catch, there are fish of over 6lb waiting to be caught for the angler with a steady nerve and some determination.

Lure fishing produces quality, if not quantity. Seb Nowosiad took this sensational fish – at just an ounce under 7lb – on a small jig.

RUDD

A lover of clear, overgrown waters, the beautiful rudd is a fish worth catching on any canal. Watching shoals of these playful fish at the surface is a truly fine way to waste a summer's afternoon. Introduce a fishing rod and it gets even better.

You won't find rudd abundant on all canals. They seem to do best in weedy places where water clarity is good. They have a wide diet and are as happy gorging on plant growth as the bugs hiding in it. The wild, shallow canals of the West Country and Ireland strike me as perfect rudd habitat: wild, undisturbed and rich in insect life. In these lush places, rudd can grow large. Indeed, it's not unusual to find specimens over a pound, and even the occasional 2-pounder on the right canal, even where the local roach barely reach half that size.

My own introduction to the world of rudd fishing began at the back of the *Double Locks Inn* on the Exeter Canal, where a tub of maggots and four metre whip provided about all the excitement a ten-year-old could handle. And what wonderful looking fish rudd are! With bright golden scales and deep red fins, they possess a deeper profile to the roach and a charm all of their own.

Quarter of a century later, these fish are still a firm summer favourite, although the fibreglass whip is usually replaced by a carbon pole or flyrod. One of the reassuring factors of rudd fishing is that it requires no elaborate equipment or bait whatsoever. Light tackle is a must, with a lightly-elasticated pole or match rod ideal. As far as getting one to bite, maggots, casters, floating bread and artificial flies all have their place.

Nor are rudd difficult to spot. Sometimes in the winter they are taken on bottom-fished baits, but the real cream of rudd fishing is from May onwards when the fish act exactly as nature intended. With a quick eye and a gaping, upturned mouth, rudd are tailor-made for feeding in the upper layers of the water.

This lifestyle lends itself perfectly to visual fishing and while you might happily plant a seat box in a single hot spot, it's even more enjoyable to don a pair of polarising glasses and travel light in search of rudd shoals.

Groups of smaller rudd can number hundreds, but for the true rudd addict, the jackpot is locating those much smaller, scarcer pockets of large fish. A fish of a pound or more represents an excellent size; a sample of double that weight would be the fish of a lifetime, an old specimen that could be the survivor of fifteen years or more.

Rudd paradise: a warm day on a neglected, rural canal.

Sunny Side Up

The techniques of catching rudd needn't be complex, but perhaps we should start with the classic weight-building methods. A waggler or pole can be used to devastating effect to present a bait up in the water. For a deadly, slow-sinking presentation, rigs often feature just one or even no shot whatsoever down the line to give a perfectly languid, natural fall of the bait.

Regular loose feed is the key to catching good weights of fish from one peg. Maggots are highly effective, but casters can form a more selective offering to pick off the better shoal fish. Bread is also a safe bet on clear canals, but this is where match and specimen disciplines part: while you might catch dozens of fish on liquidised feed and punch on a small hook, there is no finer big rudd bait than a large pinch of flake or floating crust on a size 10-12 hook.

In warm weather, floating bread is an especially exciting way to target quality rudd. Typically, I would opt to travel light with just one rod and a decent supply of bait, spending no more than half an hour in any one spot. By throwing pieces of broken bread into each swim, you'll quickly establish whether there are any good fish present. The float rig can be dispensed with entirely in this situation, with a largish piece of crust simply free-lined into the area.

Rudd are not ludicrously shy and do not generally require gossamer-thin tackle. A light float rod and 3lb line is a nice, balanced outfit. While they are not the most powerful opponents, rudd do like snaggy or weedy areas and a large one will wallow straight for the undergrowth if you let it. Awkward places definitely go with the territory and one item of tackle I'm never without when summer rudd fishing is a long-handled landing net. Without a sensible model, extracting a good fish from those absolutely prime, 'jungle' areas can be bordering on impossible unless you fancy a swim.

Prime Habitat

If there is one factor more responsible than any other in the scarcity of quality rudd on our canals, it is the ceaseless habitat destruction and alteration of waterways. Anglers are sometimes just as culpable as boat enthusiasts and local councils in their appetite for hacking back weed and plant growth to fashion open, featureless and convenient stretches of canal. In doing so, they remove both the cover and invertebrate life rudd thrive on.

Perhaps it should come as little surprise that many of my favourite rudd haunts are overgrown and neglected sections of canal. While it's true that every water benefits from some maintenance, I've had the best sport of all in rich, weedy water. It's amazing how quickly anglers will declare such swims as 'unfishable' as soon as pegged swims disappear and vegetation flourishes. But if you're prepared to travel light and get stuck in, the rudd fishing can be phenomenal.

Even the weediest quagmire can be tackled with floating bread or a fly rod. Sadly, rudd are often an easy target for poachers and they are not the hardiest fish, so the best fishing tends to be well away from access points, where casual anglers can't be bothered to walk.

We've said little of flyfishing thus far, but in terms of both selecting larger fish and the sheer pleasure of the exercise, this is my absolute favourite method. Slow-sinking wet flies such as spiders are excellent, while sunny weather is ideal to try dry flies. Virtually any small pattern

Large rudd represent the cream of high summer fishing.

Sublime viewing: a pair of plump fish hug a raft of floating weed.

will work on fine tackle, but dark and soft hackled is best. Some of the most exciting midsummer activity I've witnessed has been the rudd keying in on flying ants, and whether they're taking the real thing or not, small, dark terrestrial flies are avidly taken in humid conditions.

So my final advice to the rudd angler is to travel light and keep an open mind. If you only fish comfortable swims and miss out all the overgrown pegs, you'll only ever realise a fraction of the potential of your chosen canal. Free-lined bread can be excellent, but my best catches have been with the fly. Sessions of half a dozen or more rudd of over a pound, on light tackle, represent truly memorable sport. And best of all, rudd fishing can be brilliant on those scorching hot days that you might easily assume were better

A rudd snack: undergrowth equals insect life, such as this hawthorn fly.

for sun bathing than making a red letter catch. Hence, to my mind at least, no summer would be complete without a few afternoons chasing rudd on a quiet part of the Cut.

Right: Humid conditions and a weedy canal signal prime rudd fishing.

Flyfishing is the most exciting method of all, and often selects the bigger fish.

PIKE

The fact that our most fearsome freshwater predator is abundant on the majority of canals is lost on many who frequent the towpaths. Although sometimes maligned by match anglers, they lend a sinister presence all of their own to our canals. Pike add drama to the most sedate settings, and later they are a topic to be discussed with outstretched arm over pints of ale in waterside pubs.

Had it not been for boyhood encounters with pike on my local canal, I may never have become an avid predator angler. They form some of my keenest memories. One moment there would be a small roach or perch kicking on the line, the next a sullen, downward force and my pole rendered as useless as a child's toy. I seldom remember these mismatched battles ever ending well, beyond brief excitement and then a missing hook. I was captivated nonetheless, and can acutely remember the first time I made contact using stouter tackle, this time better equipped to take my revenge.

Does any other fish stir such emotions as the pike, or provide the canal angler with a more likely chance to catch a genuine monster? It's fair to say that in many shallower canals the pike are likely to be in the small but numerous category. Fish of two to six pounds are a great prospect for sport all the same, and you may be surprised by the occasional larger fish. The wider, deeper canals are another prospect entirely however, and those with a good head of larger prey fish such as bream can produce some exceptional pike, if you can find them. As a general rule, clearer and weedier canals hold the best populations of these fish, which tend to hunt most effectively by sight.

Left: Watching a juicy pike float is one of the highlights of the canal angler's year.

Pike Methods

A wide variety of methods work. Dead bait fishing is perhaps the most popular, but lures, flies and wobbled baits are also effective and hugely enjoyable ways to catch pike.

Whichever method you pick to take on these brilliant fish, you must show them respect. Pike inspire fear and ignorance in spades, and yet are one of the most fragile and important fish in our waters. Whether it is pollution, careless practice or illegal fishing, they always seem to be the first species to suffer.

Pike have big, greedy mouths. Striking early avoids deep hooking.

Canal Fishing

Besides strong tackle (no lighter than 15lb main line) and a wire trace, it is essential to carry adequate equipment. Foot-long forceps or specialist pliers, along with an unhooking mat are a must to remove hooks and prevent damage on the bank.

For those new to pike fishing it is also sensible policy to go with an experienced angler – and you'll also find useful tips on the Pike Anglers Club website (www.pacgb.co.uk).

Below: A piker's dawn: first light is perhaps the best time of all.

A simple floatfishing set-up works well for dead baiting on all canals.

Roving the Cut

Perhaps the best way to start fishing any canal for pike is to travel light and explore as much water as possible. Techniques are a matter of personal preference to a large extent, or at least a secondary concern to the business of location. Besides obvious places of shelter, such as sinister snags, bends and boatyards, pike will rarely be far from areas where concentrations of prey exist. In fact, the all-rounder who knows the whereabouts of roach and bream shoals on the canal is one step ahead in this regard.

In the autumn, when pike fishing begins properly, the fish can be quite evenly spread. But as temperatures cool, just as the roach shoals begin to group, the same is often true of the pike.

It is also fair to say that pike can travel fair distances on canals. It is not unheard of for a large fish to be caught twice in a season at locations a mile or more apart. The availability of food and angling pressure both have a bearing on this, and because of their popularity with casual anglers and poachers, easy access points rarely offer the best pike sport.

I routinely walk long distances in my own fishing and especially favour awkward or overgrown areas, since it's a safe bet that most other anglers will give these a miss.

Timing and conditions can also be crucial to success. Feeding spells can be short, but if I had to pick just one hour to fish for pike, it would be the first sixty minutes of daylight. Pike tend to be more active when light levels are low; their prey have less chance to see them coming at these times and the pike can capitalise on their superior eyesight. This seems especially true on clear shallow canals, where pike can prove fussy on calm sunny days.

Looking back over some twenty years of canal piking, however, I am reluctant to draw hard and fast rules about conditions. Yes, there are general rules we can observe: early and late are good times; overcast days and spells of settled weather are preferable to those periods where the temperature yo-yos up and down. There is always a chance with pike however, and with the exception of days

If you must use more than one rod, it's best to have one on a bite alarm to avoid missing runs and harming the pike.

when a thick sheet of ice covers the canal, bites are always possible. I remember catching a fine double figure pike in the middle of a sunny, calm Sunday afternoon, for example, in complete defiance of textbook logic.

Perhaps this is what makes the pike such a fascinating quarry. They are wild and unpredictable, and their moods can range from comatose to kamikaze in the span of a few hours.

On some days the only highlight will be the hot bath when you get home; on other occasions, when you find the pike active and hunting you might experience some truly unforgettable sport.

Mobile Methods

If you are relatively new to pike fishing, or indeed a particular water, perhaps the best way to start is with lure or fly tackle. For one thing, you will cover a lot of likely territory this way. Where pike are concerned, the more you seek, the more you'll find. Novices will also have fewer problems unhooking pike, as they seldom swallow artificials as they do bait.

The choice of lures available is vast, but just a handful will catch you plenty of pike. Suitable options are discussed in the dedicated chapter on lure fishing. Whichever lures or flies you use, pike fishing

> **DEAD BUT WOBBLING**
>
> Wobbling or 'sink and draw' is a deadly way to catch pike, including the biggest. Baits can be mounted on a standard pike trace with the leading treble through the lips, but a much more secure way is to use a clip. Mine are simply large snap links, where the locking arm has been straightened and sharpened (*see below*) so that it can be threaded through both lips and locked securely.
>
> 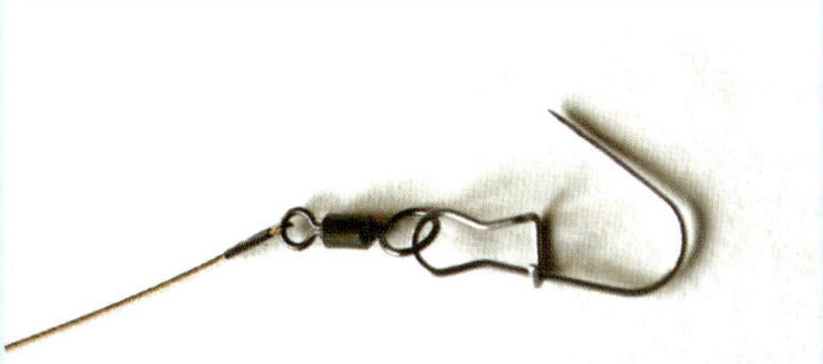
>
> *Snap link with sharpened locking arm.*
>
> 
>
> *The author's wobbling rig.*

often involves taking a few risks, because canal pike love overgrown, inaccessible places. Don't restrict yourself to potshots at the far bank either; casting parallel along the near margin is also fertile territory and pike will sometimes attack from virtually under your feet.

Flyfishing is also highly successful, and when faced with cold conditions and lazy pike, there are days when flies comfortably outfish lures. They snag less, can be fished beautifully slowly and have a subtler appeal to predators that have seen too many lures. On most canals, even a modest fly caster can reach the far bank. Nor are huge flies and shark tackle required; an eight weight and more modest sized flies no bigger than 4 inches add a degree of finesse to the experience. A simple floating flyline will suffice more often than not, although an intermediate or the addition of a sink tip can be handy for deeper canals.

My most frantic day's canal piking of all time came with game tackle, when I shared a catch of 25 pike with my brother, all on the fly. Just as brilliant as the feel of the line pulling tight in your fingers is the minimal fuss involved; a single, barbless hook can be flipped out in an instant with forceps, often without the need to take the fish from the water.

Clear, rural canals offer terrific sight fishing. Lawrence Heaton-Wright spotted this fish in shallow water, before taking aim with a bright pike fly.

A powerful fish lunges at the net: strong tackle is a must.

Thoughts on Bait

All kinds of freshwater and sea fish baits catch pike. They can also be an excellent way of singling out bigger, lazier pike, which have no qualms about scavenging an easy meal. Dead baiting needn't be a case of chuck it out and leave it, however, and there are various presentations that will work.

Wobbling or 'sink and draw' is a particular personal favourite. This is the technique of using a dead fish almost like a lure and twitching it through the water to mimic sick or dying prey. Sea fish will work, but I tend to find coarse species such as roach or small skimmers much more durable for repeated casting.

Wobbling is a great way to search the water slowly and thoroughly, giving a big pike all the time in the world to react. It is versatile too: baits can be air injected to sink painfully slowly and worked around weed growth, for example, or indeed weighted to search the depths.

If a pike follows the bait but is hesitant, you also have the option of simply letting the bait drop to the bottom to be picked up. For sheer effectiveness, sink and draw would probably be my most successful method. My first canal 20-pounder took a wobbled bait, as did my best-ever canal pike of 23lbs 10oz.

Static Presentations

Static presentations also catch plenty of pike, and while they require a little more patience there is something deliciously sinister and exciting about watching the bright tip of a large float start to bob, or line start to snake from the spool. A smelly bait such as a sardine or mackerel is also the obvious way to tackle a muddy canal where pike may struggle to find your offering by sight.

Baits needn't always sit on the bottom. Drifting or 'trotting' offerings in the tow is a fun and active way to fish.

Both float and leger presentations have their place on canals. A float set-up is ideal for weedy waters where a sunk main line is easily hindered. Legering is easier in wide or deep areas however, and the line can be kept beneath boat traffic. When I fish static rods, I like to use both methods. This way I can watch a float, while my second, legered bait is set up with a bite alarm, so I know immediately when a pike takes. Unless you have

Pike are deceptively fragile. Handle and release with care – just like Jim Moore.

Broom handle pike rods are unnecessary on typical canals. A light carp or specimen rod provides a more sporting bend.

eyes that look in different directions (not unheard of in my locality) I believe it is always safe policy to use an alarm on a second rod. Should you not detect a run, the result could be a deep-hooked pike, which is often tantamount to a dead pike. For this reason you should also stay close to your rods and hit bites early. When the line or float starts to move off, this can mean only one thing: pike don't have hands, so strike!

The part that makes the least sense in traditional pike fishing is how often we nail our baits right to the deck. For one thing, pike have eyes that look upwards. Nor are pike always glued to the canal bed; in fact, quite the opposite when hunger strikes. Legered baits can be popped up off the bottom, either by injecting them with air, or using a little balsa or foam gadget to the trace. Not only does this make your offering far more visible to the pike, it keeps it out of the weed.

Nor do float-fished baits have to be presented hard on the bottom. All canals will 'tow' through from time to time or be affected by the wind. A dead bait fished at mid-depth can be drifted to search a great deal of water and quite often outfishes one left on the deck. I like a small roach or sprat for this method, hooked through the back with just one treble to work its way along the canal. It might feel counter intuitive, but this can be a brilliant trick. The bites tend to be very positive and on shallow canals it can be a great method for the impatient pike angler to cover a lot of fish.

Perhaps I'm soft at heart, but the only method I hesitate to use is live baiting – an effective weapon no doubt, but one now banned on the majority of canals. For sensible reasons too, because every time a bucket of fish arrives from a different water, with different parasites and diseases, the angler gambles with the health of their fishery. I make no moral censure here, but should you choose to bait with live fish, you must always catch your bait from the canal you intend to fish.

Above: The jaws have it! Pete Gregory took this canal monster on a large spinnerbait.

Below: Canal pike are not always jacks! The author tempted this fine 23-pounder with a wobbled roach.

Zander have an amazing ability to hunt in conditions of poor visibility. This one managed to locate the author's fly on a muddy section of the Grand Union.

ZANDER

Love or hate them, zander are now an established feature of many British canals. Non-native they might be, but the species has a sinister charm all of its own, adding a dash of murder and intrigue to our towpaths. With an angular frame, spiked dorsal fin and fangs to boot, you would struggle to find a more thoroughly menacing predator. Although zander have spread as far south as the Gloucester Canal in recent years, the interlinked canals of the Midlands could rightly be considered the heartland of canal zander fishing, with miles of potential for the angler.

So why does their presence ignite such an adverse response? It's perfectly true that zander populations are an 'accident'. They can and do alter eco-systems, especially in the short term. But as with pike, suggestions that they 'eat everything' are simply nonsense. Like any predator, in time a stable balance is established with levels of prey fish and you won't find the one without the other.

That zander are voracious hunters is beyond doubt. Small shoal fish such as roach and bleak are particular favourites for this vampire of the fish world. The old-fashioned title of 'pike-perch' is inaccurate however, as the zander has a distinct character all of its own.

The Way of the 'Zed'

Taking a cursory glance at the typical canals where zander proliferate, it's little surprise they do well. Their large eyes give them a big advantage in conditions of low visibility, hence urban areas where the bottom is continually stirred up with boats suit them perfectly.

A smaller head than the pike betrays a killer that prefers numerous, smaller meals. So is it any surprise that canals teeming with one ounce roach, perch and

Zander are a deadly and unpredictable quarry to add to your species list.

Lure angler John Cheyne took this fine beast with a soft lure presented close to the bank.

bleak make such happy hunting grounds?

Zander might display impressive dentistry, but their habits are very different to pike. They are roving, pack hunters rather than solitary ambush predators, although the large zander become loners. These habits already yield clues to zander location. While you might think of searching different 'lairs' for pike, the zander fisher often thinks more in terms of patrol routes. Junctions, connecting arms, bridges, bays and boatyards are all places where a well-aimed bait or lure is likely to be intercepted by zander as they move between areas.

The other giveaway is any place where prey fish congregate. Find any concentration of small roach, skimmers or bleak and you can bet that the zander will carry out regular raids.

Zander particularly like the sloping shelf on each side of a canal too, using these like corridors on a waterway. In murky water or at times of low light, however,

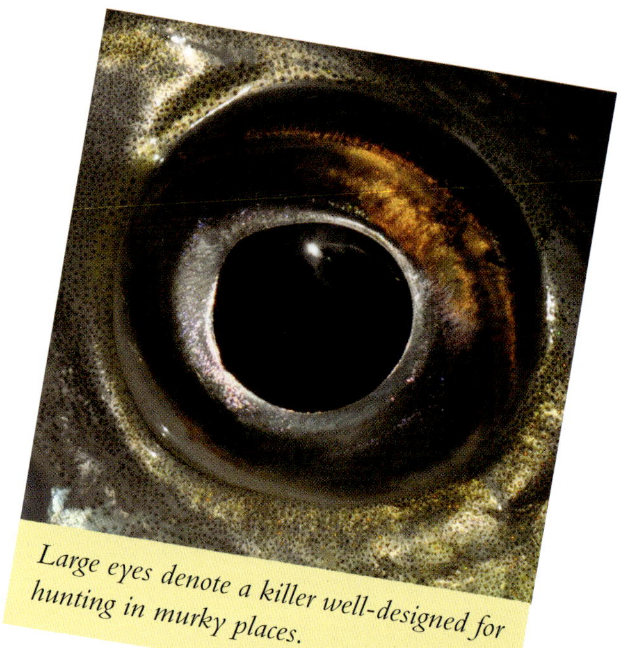

Large eyes denote a killer well-designed for hunting in murky places.

they will venture right into the shallows to go on the attack. Dull days, evenings or even night times tend to be productive for zander fishing, but this idiosyncratic hunter is far from predictable. Bites can arrive in the middle of a sunny day as well as the dead of night and this is in essence part of their allure. Zander fishing is a matter of not only location, but experimentation and fine-tuning methods.

A potent groundbait mix with chopped fish helps to draw in predators.

Dead and Loving It

Various methods will catch zander, but bait fishing is the first port of call for many anglers hoping to attract and tempt zander in the murk of a busy canal. It makes perfect sense to offer them what they are already looking for, namely small coarse fish. Locating and catching a few of these can be a worthwhile exercise in itself, since concentrations of juvenile silver fish will also often reveal areas where zander like to dine. A whip is ideal, along with tiny hooks and baits such as pinkies to select the smaller samples.

Live baits will certainly work, but many waters ban this practice. I must confess I also dislike live baiting, and in any case have found a small dead fish is seldom refused and much easier to present in a tidy fashion. Typically such offerings are much smaller than pike baits, to accommodate the zander's comparatively smaller mouth. A roach, rudd, skimmer or bleak of 5-8cm is perfect, although somewhat bigger baits can be cut into bite-sized sections.

Zander can be surprisingly picky feeders, so large crude treble hooks and

ZANDER RIG REFINEMENTS

A simple running leger rig works perfectly for zander, but I also like to add some refinements. One of these is to replace the lead with an open-end swimfeeder, into which I pack a mixture of fishmeal-based crumb groundbait along with chopped fish pieces. I firmly believe that this helps zander home in on my bait. Another tweak is to incorporate a small piece of foam near the hook to gently 'pop up' your dead bait. A split shot then anchors the bait to the bottom. This is especially useful on debris-strewn canals or those with regular boat disturbance, where casts can be wasted by unwanted crud ruining presentation.

Small deadbaits are best for zander, while a feeder improves the scent trail.

thick wire are not ideal for traces. Wire is essential to prevent bite-offs and accidentally-hooked pike, however. Modern, ultra-supple wires are perhaps the best compromise, together with small barbless treble hooks. Another alternative that is kinder to your quarry than two trebles is to hair rig a small fish using just a single size 4-6 carp hook.

Zander are rightly renowned for their dislike of resistance. When legering, a 'drop off' system can be used as you might employ for pike, whereby the line pulls from a clip on the take and the fish can then run off freely. However, I much prefer to have the rod at an angle and watch the tip for bites, much like a quivertip angler. This system of laying the rod more or less parallel to the bank also suits many towpaths, which can be limited in terms of space, as well as rather hard to push bank sticks into.

In terms of rods for bait fishing, zander are not the strongest opponents and can easily come adrift using overgunned tackle. It's also desirable to use a rod that will give a satisfying bend with the average canal zander, which will often be under four pounds in weight. A light specimen or avon rod of 1¼-1½lbs test curve is ideal, or even a barbel rod with a coloured tip section to detect takes. Line strengths should be a minimum of 10lbs, but I much prefer 20lb braid.

The best advice I can give with bites is to strike promptly. As soon as you get a positive pull on the rod tip, just strike. Zander can be quite gentle in this respect, certainly less full-blooded than pike. If you delay there are two possible outcomes: a dropped bait or a deeply hooked zander, neither of which are desirable. You will never connect with every bite, but those missed are likely to be the smallest 'school' fish, not the bigger ones that have no trouble devouring a fingerling roach in a split second. I would rather strike promptly and miss the odd small fish than risk hooks being swallowed, which could kill your quarry.

Lures and Mobile Methods

Another popular way to catch zander is with a light lure fishing outfit. This has the added advantage of mobility, which is a real plus for any new water or one with few obvious features, where you are not sure where the fish will turn up.

Zander are certainly excellent at detecting prey in unsavoury conditions and much of the time it is the angler's confidence that suffers in murky water, rather than the zander's uncanny ability to locate the target. In fact my lure angling friend John Cheyne has had some hectic action with lures just after a boat has passed through lock gates, the sudden increase in water colour and movement serving to disorientate bait fish and give zander the perfect opportunity to go on the offensive. That said, the fishing often gets easier from October onwards, when boat traffic slows down and autumn rainwater freshens up the canal, making for slightly better clarity and active fish.

As with bait fishing tactics, tackle and lures tend to be scaled down for zander fishing. A light lure fishing rod with a crisp tip section is ideal for working lures in the

The author fishes a junction between canals, a likely passing point for zander.

2-3 inch bracket and enjoying a good scrap with the typical 'school' zander of 2-3lb. Traditional diving plugs and spinners can work, but the most widely effective zander lure is the more modern soft 'shad' style jig. These can be worked slowly and 'jigged' across the deck with little twitches of the rod tip where required – and it is almost always the bottom foot of water where the zander will be found. Models with a single, upturned hook are ideal for canal fishing as they pick up less debris than other models. More notes on this method can be found in the chapter on lure fishing.

Drop-shotting is another alternative, and you can even combine a conventional jig on the end of your trace with a small drop shot lure a foot or so higher on the line to effectively cover two levels in the water.

There is no substitute for a top quality braided line when zander fishing, which is superior in terms of strength, sensitivity and casting performance. It is vital to keep in touch with the lure at all times and 'feel' what it is doing. Zander experts often use coloured braids too and watch the line for suspicious movements, as zander will sometimes take gently or move straight towards the angler.

Less fashionable 'mobile' methods for zander also include flyfishing and wobbling. Flyfishing can be terrific fun and my own zander patterns often feature dumbell eyes to make the pattern fish 'point up' like a jig, and I've also tried incorporating small rubber tails to help the fish home in.

Wobbling seems seldom used for zander, but the 'fireball' rig is well worth a try: this is the practice of presenting a small deadbait on jig head, usually with a small length of wire attached to fasten a 'stinger' treble towards the tail end of the fish. The bait is then fished rather like a jig, the angler letting it sink to the bottom and then making a series of twitches on the rod tip to jig its way through likely areas, lifting and dropping back down attractively. The real fish has the added advantage that a biting zander will often hang on for longer, giving the angler more time to strike.

While not strictly necessary, night fishing for zander can add a certain drama! Here, the author tries the Birmingham and Fazeley Canal under the lights of suburbia.

Further Notes

Zander are one of the most fascinating species of all for the canal specialist, but one with plenty of enemies on our waterways. Technically speaking, under byelaws, they are not meant to be released when captured. I advise you to ignore this totally stupid rule. Zander are now a sustainable part of freshwater ecosystems, which find their niche alongside other fish species. They add a welcome mystery to many canals, a genuine challenge and are a firm favourite with predator anglers.

Zander are here to stay. Eliminating them from our canals is totally unrealistic, so we might as well accept and enjoy them. I would go further, in fact, urging anglers to handle and release these fish carefully. Like pike, they demand both respect and correct unhooking tools (long-nosed pliers at minimum).

While the typical canal zander is often a modest creature in size, there is also a growing potential for the specimen hunter. Any fish over 4lb should be regarded as a fine canal zander, while the record stands at a mighty 17lb, from the Ashby Canal.

It is my belief that most well-established Cuts have the occasional double-figure beast lurking in them. Regardless of what the authorities say, these are fish to be treasured and carefully released. A large zander is a thing of spectacular and sinister beauty, not vermin or something to go with chips.

GUDGEON

There might be those among the readers of this book who will wonder why I have given the diminutive gudgeon his own little chapter. Can I be serious? Yes, deadly serious. They are beautiful little fish. Colourful, free-biting and fun, gudgeon are a delight to any true angler.

'Gonks', 'gobios', call them what you will, gudgeon are one of Britain's forgotten coarse fish. Populations have diminished and anglers have become too obsessed with pounds and ounces to worry about such a small fish. And yet in more innocent moments of our past they were highly valued. We once ate them, treasured them and even held gudgeon fishing parties.

In the not-so-distant past, gudgeon fishing was refined into an art form by match anglers looking for winning weights on hard canals. When you consider that the average 'gonk' weighs next to nothing, you start to appreciate the kind of feat catching half a stone of the whiskery little blighters represents.

And what splendid creatures they are. Anything but 'brown' as some books describe them, look closely at the gudgeon and you'll find a brocade of silver, blue and gold. They also give a pleasant, juddering fight on light tackle such as a whip and will eagerly take just about any bait they can fit in their whiskery mouths, which are pretty big considering the tiny size of the fish.

Catching gudgeon from a canal is refreshingly simple. They can be widely distributed on certain canals and are not fussy. The canal angler in search of gudgeon-based gratification needn't look

Gudgeon fanatic Neil Williams displays a typical canal 'gonk'.

far from the bank to catch them, for starters. They occupy the central track avidly, but are also present in the shallowest water right by the bank in all but the bitterest of the seasons. The short pole or whip is king, along with a lightish rig and regular helpings of maggots, pinkies or squats. The match men of the past would also mix up plenty of potent dark groundbait, often with a slightly bitter edge, and add a little thumbnail sized chunk at regular intervals to start what might be described as a 'gobio frenzy'.

If you find the fish in numbers however, do be kind. By setting your bait at dead depth, hitting bites early and going barbless, you'll have plenty of fun without harming these speckled little beasties.

DID YOU KNOW?

In old English, the word 'gudgeon' was slang for a person who is easily fooled, owing to their greediness to bite at anything edible.

The gudgeon: a fish to delight all ages.

Members of GUGGS (The Grand Union Canal Gobio Gobio Society) while away a sunny afternoon in fine style.

Gobio Mania

So where exactly would we place the gudgeon in today's fishing landscape? Perhaps these fish are enjoying a quiet resurgence as anglers grow jaded with stocked fisheries which do little to remind them of childhood.

One of the most delightful of detours in the making of this book was a fishing trip with members of GUGGS, or 'The Grand Union Gobio Gobio Society' to give them their rather splendid full title. Having grown tired of ultra-serious fishing and size obsession, Neil Williams and some pals set up their own specialist club to cater for the gudgeon enthusiast. An astounding total of over four hundred members include Keith Arthur and Bill Rushmer. The grand sum of 50p will gain you entrance into one of the club's sweepstake matches, where a row of red float tips bob and each wriggling fish swung to hand is met with hoots of excitement.

The ultimate target for this band of enthusiasts is a 'thirty'. Where the humble gudgeon is concerned, a fish of thirty grams represents a true canal specimen.

Such creatures are talked of with fervour by GUGGS members over pints of real ale, and the captor of such a beast is given the honour of naming the fish to be immortalized in the club's hall of fame.

Each calendar year has a specific letter, so for example the giant (in relative terms) gudgeon list of 2013 includes Kylie, Kipper and Klingon.

Fittingly enough, club founder Neil Williams is the current UK canal record holder with a giant fish of 45.9 grams named 'Hugh Mungous'. You really couldn't make it up, or indeed spend a happier afternoon than stealing a few hours to go gudgeon fishing.

Beauty is in the eye – or should that be the hand? – of the beholder. In this case: Phil Madley.

Silver bream – a species found in many UK canals. It can be distinguished from the common (or bronze) bream by dark, almost blackish-edged fins and a comparatively big eye.

OTHER SPECIES

One of the genuine charms of fishing on any of Britain's canals is the fact that the next bite could be almost anything. We might have dealt with the most commonly-occurring and most popular species in depth, but a complete list of fish found in canals would be a much longer and more bizarre one.

How do creatures as diverse as flounders and koi carp get into our waterways? Fish are introduced in many ways. As well as official, legal stocking programmes, there are numerous accidental and incidental transferrals of fish; such as when rivers connect to man-made waters, or winter floods scatter stock between waters. Of course, there are also many wholly illegal ways fish become established, from shifty anglers sneaking carp or catfish into waters, to discarded pets.

Just a handful of examples illustrate how canals can throw up some truly eye-opening catches. Barbel have found their way into relief channels and been landed on several occasions, along with the odd salmon; a winter match on the Bude Canal was once won with a large flounder. My personal most remarkable 'accidental' capture took place on the Huddersfield Broad Canal, where I caught a stunning, 1½lb wild brown trout from one of the most urban, gritty sections of water I've ever fished.

So where might we begin with a lowdown of additional canal species and unwanted guests? Some species are certainly more common (and desirable) than others, so we'll start with these. For those keen to target the unusual, a scan through the reference section on British canals will also make interesting reading, where unusual species and individual captures are noted.

Dace

A classic flowing-water species, dace are nevertheless present in quite a few of our canals. Any channels that connect to natural streams and rivers at some point in their length are likely to feature the odd shoal of this pretty silver fish.

In the Exeter Canal near the River Exe, for example, you can see these fish chasing just under the surface in the spring. Until you have watched their slender forms close up, you might easily think these were roach, but it is not so.

Dace tend to be caught in the upper layers of the water on canals, and if present are likely to respond to similar 'on the drop' tactics that you might use for roach and rudd. Maggots, casters and bread punch are all good baits.

Eels

They might not be everyone's favourite fish, but even in the current decline of eel stocks, canals can be excellent venues to catch the species. They can be found in just about every canal to some extent. Rivers are one obvious supply line, but one of the strangest things I have ever witnessed was an eel making its way through flooded grass towards the Exeter Ship Canal.

Eels were once prized by match anglers and indeed, when the going is tough, liberal feeding with dead maggots or chopped worm is a good strategy. Tackle should be a little stronger than typical match fishing fare, with plenty of spare hooklengths tied for inevitable losses. I still remember playing a good one for several minutes before losing the fish that would comfortably have won me the weekly match.

Pete Gregory used a small deadbait in the black of night to tempt this 4lb canal eel.

The potential for large eels is also there on canals and a huge fish could go uncaught for many years. Deep, snaggy areas are a good bet with a small dead bait or bunch of worms, although they will come in closer at night, which is prime time to catch a good fish. Tackle should be robust, with 15lb main line and wire traces the order of the day, because big eels can destroy conventional hook links.

Bleak

Another common silver fish that occurs naturally in many canals and, like dace, favour the upper layers of the water. They are easy to catch and just as easy to identify, their lower lip pointing upwards rather like a miniature tarpon.

Admittedly, they will be only of passing interest to most anglers, although for match fishers and youngsters they can offer bite-a-chuck fishing where present, using fine float tackle and maggots. They can also signal the whereabouts of predators; on the Kennet and Avon Canal, for example, I once found an area teeming with these fish that proved to be an excellent pike spot.

Trout

You could spend a long time looking for trout on a typical canal, but it very much depends on the setting. The once-in-a-decade freak capture is one thing, but some canals have a sizeable population of brown trout. The most reliable trout fishing on canals is surely in Scotland: the

It sounds like a euphemism, but this Huddersfield trout came from the grittiest of canal settings – much to my complete astonishment.

Caledonian Canal has many brownies, which come from the adjoining lochs.

Rural Wales also has the odd canal trout, as do some English canals that connect to streams and rivers. Not all are tiny, greedy things either and the Lee Navigation, to give just one example, has occasionally thrown up large trout.

Where reasonable populations are encountered, these greedy fish are not hard to catch. Flies or spinners are fun ways to proceed, but the fastest way to see if there are trout present is with a simple float-fished worm.

Silver Bream

Often misidentified as skimmers (small common bream), the silver bream is marked by its smaller size, dark fins and comparatively large eye.

They are only present in some canals, but probably more widespread than popularly thought. They are present in parts of the Grand Union for example, but for sheer numbers the best water that I know of is the Taunton to Bridgwater Canal. Pretty fish they are too.

Silver bream respond well to small baits and little and often feeding. I've taken them on maggots and even wet flies, but given reasonable water clarity, perhaps the best method of all for canal fishing is bread punch. Like roach, they like a small bait fished just touching the deck. Pole tackle or a canal waggler dotted right down is ideal to spot the shy bites they give. The smaller fish sometimes take on the drop, although the best samples usually come on the bottom. Any fish above half a pound represents a good one.

Crucian Carp

Crucians are an angler's favourite wherever found. They do extremely well on canals, and where clubs control sections of water that are smaller, enclosed pounds, stocks

Crucian carp put in a cheeky appearance on a select few canals.

can be safely contained. Perhaps the best crucian canal in Britain is the Newport in Shropshire, where the usual rules for this cute, cagey species apply. Pole fished baits such as corn, caster and maggot fished on sensitive tackle are ideal.

Barbel

Now we're really starting to lose the plot! But is the idea of barbel on canals really so outrageous? These powerful fish certainly do find their way through lock gates and connecting channels. Winter floods are a particular time when things get mixed up and barbel seek to escape main flows, finding their way into canals and relief channels more often than you think.

The fishing world did an almighty double take in 2009, when the *Angling Times* reported the capture of a 16lb barbel from the Oxford Canal near Banbury. Remarkably, pleasure angler Alan Holmes played the fish for some fifteen minutes on the pole. Although an accidental catch, this is by no means the only canal barbel landed. It would take a brave, or mad, angler to specifically target them from a towpath however.

Salmon and Sea Trout

Perhaps even more bonkers than canal barbel, migratory game fish do also turn up once in a blue moon. Again, canals and relief channels which form detours on river courses are the locations where the impossible does occasionally happen. Less surprising is their presence in the Highlands, where the Caledonian Canal connects sea-bound lochs. Local legend has it that a small boy caught a big sea trout at the top of 'Neptune's Staircase' by idly flicking a spinner above the top lock gate.

Let's be honest though, as fascinating as such captures are, salmon fishing is temperamental enough without throwing a canal into the mix!

Ruffe

One of Britain's forgotten, sadly declining species, the ruffe nevertheless still finds sanctuary on several of our canals. Such is its rare status these days that any capture should be regarded as something rather special. Where present, pole or whip fished maggots or worm sections are as likely method as any to make contact with this small, speckled, perch-like fish, which those of the older generations still get rather nostalgic about.

Another forgotten species, ruffe are a catch to be celebrated.

Catfish can go (or should that be 'grow') undetected for years on canals.

Catfish

Wherever there are dodgy anglers, maverick species can crop up. And with the catfish we find here, the wels, being an adaptable, long-lived and highly predatory species, the potential is there for the odd monster in years to come. Whether or not this is a good thing is open to debate. Those responsible rarely seem to appreciate the effect an invasive species can have on an ecosystem, and while Britain might be rather cool for these fish to spawn, global warming could see a rise in catfish populations, which would have a direct effect on our native predators such as pike, to say nothing of bream, roach and other prey species. Strictly speaking, any catfish landed in a British canal should be retained and a phone call made to the Environment Agency.

But where does the catfish trail lead us? The freak appearance of a 16lb 15oz catfish proved a match winner for Nick Darke on the Grand Union Canal at Marsworth in 2011. But equally, for every authenticated capture there must be a dozen rumours. The Leeds to Liverpool and Exeter Ship Canals are just two locations where stories of big cats have been simmering. To catch one of these fish could require an endless amount of hours with large, smelly offerings such as halibut pellets or deadbaits. The truth is out there somewhere.

Goldfish, Koi & Ornamentals

The appearance of fish that would look more at home in a garden pond or aquarium is a classic, if sadly familiar story on canals across the land. Virtually every canal within spitting distance of a town or city has its stray species, escapees released by locals in most cases.

Anything but drab, the golden rudd (above) is a beautiful quirk of nature.

Several coarse species will hybridise. The roach/bream hybrid is the most common, but other results are freakier. My best guess at the fish in this picture is a rudd/bream hybrid (a 'brudd' you might say).

Goldfish have been taken on many canals and the story I received from David Stevens is typical:

I had a great day at the funfair, aged about ten, but couldn't persuade my folks that our home wouldn't be complete without the fourteen goldfish I'd won. As we went home I was ordered to put them all in the canal. I kicked off a bit, but thirteen of them were released. About three years later, I was allowed to go fishing on the canal with a couple of mates in the exact same spot. One day along with the small bits and pieces we were catching, were three goldfish, all of which had grown to about a pound!

Fun-fair prizes are not the only escapees either: large koi have also been taken on the Chester, Regents and many other canals and the odd one can be found on virtually any man-made waterway where populations of carp exist. Ide have been legally stocked in some waters; and canals such as the Lancaster contain some large grass carp.

Are less legitimate stocks a threat? Probably not, in terms of competing with wild fish. But the very real danger comes from the spread of parasites and diseases from these invaders. The odd genuine surprise certainly adds some novelty to the local canal, and it's also fair to say that not every one of these freak captures is unnatural. Perhaps the most obvious example of a beautiful, but natural, freak would be the golden rudd. Where large populations of the wild natives exist, every so often a heavily pigmented fish will occur. These beauties can be carrot-orange in coloration, making them beautiful to look at but also a magnet for predators.

POLE FISHING

If there is one piece of fishing tackle synonymous with canal fishing, it must surely be the long pole. Some things in life were just made for one another: is it any coincidence that our standard long pole measures in at between eleven and thirteen metres, pretty much bang on the width of our typical canal?

In the right hands, it is a deadly method. Those without a pole are missing out on our canals. Perhaps we should start by dismissing a few clichés: pole fishing takes a little getting used to but is not a difficult method. Nor is it for small fish only. Modern poles are far stronger as well as lighter than those we once used, and are commonly used for species such as carp and tench. They are also cheaper, and a decent quality pole is now an affordable reality for any angler.

Why is a pole regarded as the 'go to' method for so many canal anglers? Put simply, there are things you can do with a pole that you would never manage with a rod and reel. Because there is no reel or casting involved, pole tackle can be exceedingly sensitive and delicate. It offers total control, whether that means keeping your bait still in a breeze, plumbing the depth accurately or hitting the shyest bite from a roach or skimmer. With a pole, you can lower a bait right beside a tempting-looking snag or introduce a ball of groundbait as accurately as you could have placed it by hand. All these factors add up to an extremely effective method.

Pole Basics

The pole that is just right for your own fishing, not to mention your wallet, is a matter of careful choice. You don't need to break the bank, but it's worth taking your local canal into account as well as what you can afford. A lot of typical British canals are between 11 and 13 metres wide, making it well worth investing in a longer model. As with any fishing tackle you get what you pay for, but a perfectly useable pole of this length needn't cost you a fortune.

Mail order deals and second hand offers are worth considering, but nothing beats getting to your local tackle shop and actually balancing a pole in your own hands. You want something you can comfortably fish with, but it's also worth looking for deals. These shops want your business so try and seek out a package that gives you some spares and sundries as well as just the basic pole itself.

Have a look at any long pole and you will see it comes in a series of hollow sections that are stored inside one another. These sections are numbered so that number one is the final, thinnest tip section, whereas higher numbers will be the progressively thicker middle and 'butt' sections tapering to the opposite end.

Top of the list of spares for most pole anglers would be at least one additional 'top three kit.' These final tip sections of pole are where you will attach your line and having more than one to work with is a big advantage on the bank. For example, you might have a roach fishing rig on a light 'top three' kit, but you may well have a stronger top three kit set up for targeting larger fish such as tench or carp in the same session. Having additional 'top kits' allows you to switch rigs quickly and easily.

These top two or three sections contain an internal elastic to help cushion the fight of the fish (simply google 'elasticating a pole' or better still, ask at your local tackle shop). A typical pole rig will be roughly the same length as the final three pole sections, so that fish can be easily swung in or netted. There are variations however: for a really shallow margin swim, for example, you might only need a rig as long as two sections; for really deep water on ship canals your rig could be as long as four or five pole sections.

Long poles are described as 'take apart' meaning these sections are literally detached or connected by the angler while fishing. This adding or removing of pole sections is often called 'shipping' the pole. The angler

Dominic's Tip

Are you sitting comfortably?
Pole fishing shouldn't feel like a strain and this is where organisation and practice come in. You should try to keep sit comfortably upright, with your knees roughly level with your backside – a seat box with adjustable legs helps with comfort.

Try to keep everything you need to hand, so that you don't need to stoop or stretch while holding the pole. Side trays, rests, bait waiters and other accessories help here.

With practice you can stay comfy but in full control. By trapping your pole between thigh and forearm *(see photo below)* it is possible to free the hands for throwing or catapulting bait in. Bites can still be struck by lifting the knee.

A fish nears the bank as the pole is shipped back.

might add every available section to 'ship' his or her pole out to the far bank, for example, or use half the sections available to fish midway across the canal.

On a quiet lake or river, a pole angler might be able to 'ship' an entire pole in or out with all the sections attached, only ever removing the final three sections with the rig attached. This is done by sliding the pole between the hands and passing it forwards or backwards. Canals are busy places however. Pedestrians and bicycles can make it a dangerous business to pass several metres of carbon through the air. To avoid accidents, most canal anglers will remove sections in manageable chunks: for example, taking off two sections at a time. Canal anglers will often lay these sections parallel to the bank where they won't obstruct the towpath or be trodden on. Another common practice is to bring the pole in sideways, rather than directly behind where it might get damaged by others using the towpath.

On busy canals, it is good practice to ship and store pole sections and top kits parallel to the bank, rather than onto the path where they might be damaged. A pole roller helps assist with shipping, as well as keeping precious pole sections raised where they won't get chipped or dirty (or alternatively, laying pole sections on a soft bag or unhooking mat will also help protect them when not in use).

Pole Craft

Working a canal swim with the pole is very much a case of keeping your options open and trying various areas or 'lines' with different rigs and baits. Effective pole anglers rarely put all their eggs in one basket, and instead use different lengths of pole to find the fish and explore alternatives. By trickling bait accurately into two or more areas, the angler can quickly switch to find the fish. The next bite could arrive right on the far shelf of the canal, slap bang down the middle or indeed just off the keepnet on the near bank. The best pole anglers on canals are experts at juggling different options to make the most from one swim or 'peg'.

While a top match angler might try up to half a dozen different 'lines' in a session, the easiest option for the pleasure angler is to start with just a couple of alternatives. For example, fishing light and close in for roach and perch on one line, while also feeding the far bank to try later for bigger fish such as bream and tench. Even if you're only fishing for fun, it's useful to have a plan B in case your first area doesn't work or bites slow down.

A range of different baits and rigs makes perfect sense for the pole angler, who might start the session catching small roach on pinkies but might later switch to fishing casters or worms further out to add bigger 'bonus fish' to the catch. The skill is in knowing how to get the best out of the swim, feeding carefully and doing everything methodically and accurately.

The Right Moves

One of the biggest advantages of pole fishing is the sheer control and delicacy involved. There is simply no cuter way of positioning and manipulating a baited rig. Consider the difference, for example, between a waggler or feeder splashing down in shallow water; or a fine pole rig,

ONE SWIM, MANY OPTIONS

The precise nature of pole fishing makes it ideal for testing every likely corner of a swim with unerring accuracy. It is very much a process of trying different options and switching baits and rigs to keep bites coming. Feeding is absolutely vital, and by having different areas to try you can experiment.

It also pays to leave a decent gap between different 'lines' on the canal. Not only does this keep areas separate, but prevents fish spooking. For example, when you hook a fish on the far bank, you don't want to bring it directly through another area you've been feeding. There are exceptions to every rule, however: I often like to fish pinkies for small roach, but also introduce hempseed just a meter or so further to give an area for their bigger shoal-mates to settle.

A pole is ideal for lowering baits precisely to features on the far bank.

gently lowered into position. Which is most likely to touch down in the exact spot every time, without scaring the fish?

Pole anglers don't 'cast', strictly speaking, but simply lower or 'lay out' their rig (typically by gently swinging the rig out to one side and letting everything settle naturally). They also have the distinct advantage of being able to reposition or manipulate their rigs with small, deft movements. One typical trick is to lift the pole tip slightly to make the bait rise and settle again. Skilled pole anglers do this often and it's amazing how frequently a fish will notice the movement and take the bait just as it settles. With several metres of pole in your hands, every movement is magnified, hence only a very small movement is required.

Pole fishing isn't for small fish only, as Dave Sellick demonstrates with a cracking bag of canal tench and bream.

MAGIC MARKERS

Accuracy is key when pole fishing. One way to hit the same exact spot every time is to pick a 'marker' with which to line up your pole. This could be a branch or post on the far bank, for example. Your aim is to keep your loose feed and rig in one tight area consistently. If you can concentrate the fish, so much the better.

The same is true of striking with the pole. That eleven metres or so is like a giant lever, making the smallest lift capable of setting the hook. It's a good job they've become lighter, but the sight of a row of anglers grimacing over their lengths of carbon is still an endearing image of canal fishing in Britain. Nevertheless, with practice and a modern long pole, fishing at distance can be comfortable as well as deadly. And with practice, anglers can still feed bait, eat a sandwich or roll a cigarette while retaining full control.

Playing fish is a matter of steady control. From the stretch of elastic you'll quickly get an idea of the size of fish you've hooked. In the case of a smaller fish, your first move should be to draw it smoothly away from its shoal mates to avoid spooking them.

Bigger fish will need more tiring out, although playing it steady is often better than a sharp pull in the early stages, which can cause your adversary to power off angrily.

Perhaps the riskiest stage of the fight is when you break down the pole to remove sections, so try to do this smoothly, with the elastic well stretched.

The pole tip is often kept up during the fight, but you can also use a low tip to draw a fish away from the far bank or even to sink the line under trailing branches or other snags. The one thing you mustn't do is point the pole at the fish, which could cause the pole sections to separate!

Pole Elastics

In its use of special elastics, pole fishing represents a unique way of playing and landing fish. While conventional running line anglers use a combination of rod flex and the reel's drag to land fish, a pole doesn't bend to the same extent and most of the tension of the fight is handled by internally-fitted elastic. Your choice of elastic is down to the fishing you do, but there isn't such a thing as 'one size fits all.' A thick elastic would be too harsh for catching small roach, just as a fine elastic would be too weak to stop a large, powerful fish such as a carp or tench.

The choice of pole elastics is wide, but can generally be broken into two types:

Solid elastics are a basic and effective option for various sizes of fish and strengths of tackle. A simple number rating gives a basic guide, and the higher the number the thicker and more robust the elastic will be. The really light stuff, in numbers 1-3 was once favoured for catching small fish in tough conditions, but is rarely used these days. Nevertheless, light to mid range elastics from sizes 4-6 are still useful for catching small-to-mid-sized fish such as roach, perch and skimmers. The advantage of relatively fine elastics is their forgiving nature: they don't snap back too quickly or crudely, making it easy to hook and land smaller fish smoothly.

Going up through the numbers, heavier elastics handle heavier rigs and more demanding circumstances. A

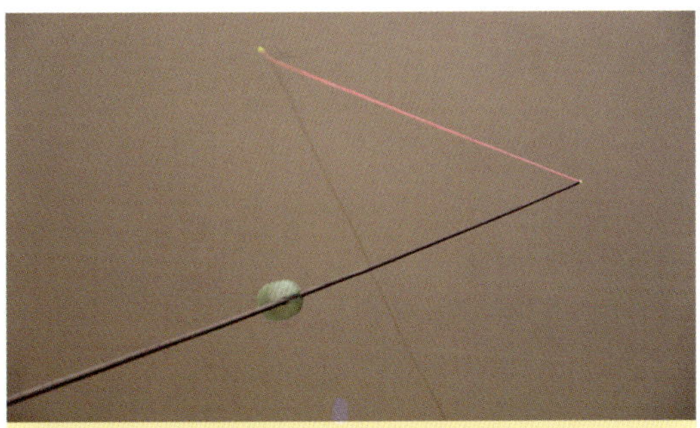

Elastic stretches to contain a good fish (the elastic connector can be picked out in yellow). Guiding better fish steadily is often better than using shock tactics.

number 8, for example, would be ideal for a canal where adult bream, larger perch or fish such as crucians might make an appearance. Higher numbers of 10 and above would be suitable for harder battlers like tench and chub. The table *(opposite)* should give a rough idea of applications.

While you have a bit of leeway with elastics, there is nothing like having just the right tool for the job. You might still catch roach on a heavier grade, for example, but a common issue will be that the smaller fish get 'bumped' on the strike, because the elastic is rather robust for the job.

With lighter elastics the opposite problem occurs – you might land a large, ponderous bream on a number 4-6 for example, but a powerful fish such as a tench would give you minimal control.

Hollow elastics are perhaps the best compromise when you want to catch small and large fish on the same rig. These are more expensive, but possess added stretch and durability. They are noticeably thicker than traditional, solid elastics, but have more 'give'. The lightest of them are ideal for catching both average-sized shoal fish but also stopping the odd larger party crasher (that said, I would still pick a solid number 4-6 elastic for catching

BALANCING A FINE BRISTLE

Ultra-fine pole bristles can be excellent detecting for shy bites, but a bit of a nightmare to keep proud of the surface. One useful dodge is to apply a touch of Mucilin or Vaseline to keep the very tip showing. If you forget these, you could also use the natural grease from the sides of your nose (no kidding – it works!)

Dominic's Tip

Elastic is threaded through pole sections and secured at either end by a bright connector at the tip, and a bung at the rear. The design pictured has a little winder that adjusts tension easily. The bung is stored inside the pole and can be retrieved with a hooked wire length. If you ever lose this tool or get the bung stuck, the easiest cure is to put some five-minute epoxy glue on a thin stick and push this into the bung. When the glue dries you can pull the bung free.

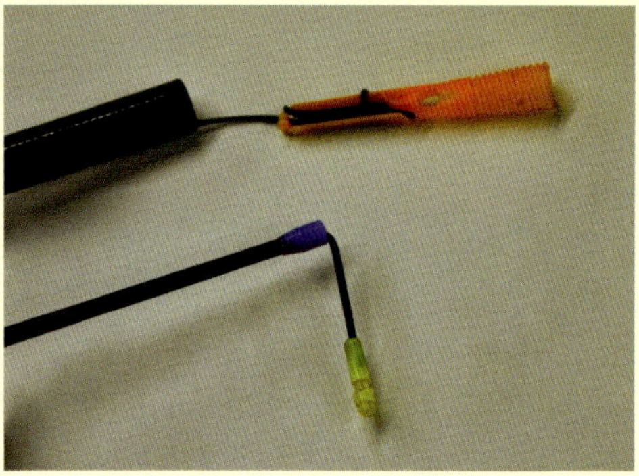

Elastic Rating	Rig Strength	Typical Species
1-3	Lines down to 1lb, hooks 20-24	Roach, perch, gudgeon, 'bits'
4	Lines 1-2lb, hooks 18-22	Roach, rudd, perch, skimmers
6	Lines 1½-2lb hooks 16-20	Roach, rudd, perch, skimmers & bream
8	Lines 2-3lb hooks 12-18	Bream, larger roach & perch, chub, crucians
10-12	Lines 3-4lb hooks 10-14	Tench, chub, big perch, small carp
12-18	Lines 4-6lb hooks 10-14	Carp, tench, large chub, any big fish around snags

roach and skimmers). The thicker grades are superb for battling tench, chub and carp but are also soft enough to handle more docile, softer-mouthed fish such as bream. Various companies have their own differing colour-coded strengths, so do pick carefully.

The tension of the elastic can also be crucial. In open water areas with smaller fish, for example, you could set elastics quite gently to provide plenty of give so that species such as roach don't wriggle off the hook easily. At the other end of the scale, fishing to snags demands thicker elastics set tighter. With large perch or chub hooked beside snags, for example, you can't afford to let the fish run, hence you want a heavier elastic that provides plenty of initial resistance.

Elastics should usually be set up so that the connector returns smoothly but snugly to the pole tip. Loose elastic protruding is bad news. Cutting and re-tying is one answer to this loss of tension, but better still is to use a bung that allows the elastic to be carefully tensioned.

One final point: regardless of which elastic you use, apply some lubricant. Various types are widely available and should be applied directly to the elastic as you stretch it from the pole tip before fishing. One cheap solution is watered down washing up liquid, which literally can be poured down the tip of your pole as you give the elastic a pull, for maximum lubrication.

DEPTH MARKERS

Whether you use correction fluid or a little sleeve, it's well worth marking the exact depth onto your pole. This way, should you want to come shallower or move overdepth, you can always return to your starting depth.

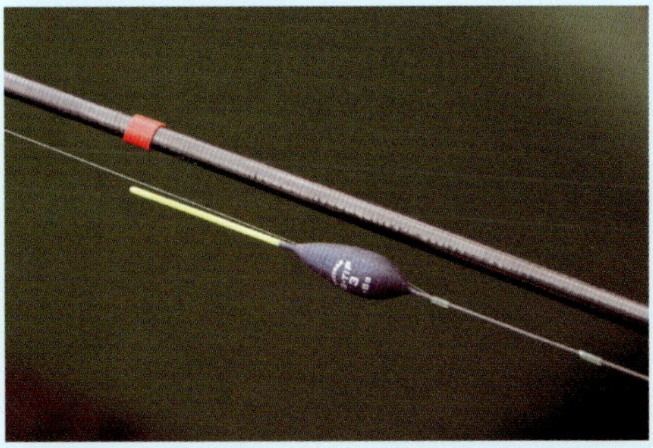

ANATOMY OF A POLE RIG

Creating perfect rigs for various uses is essential preparation for any pole angler. Shop-bought rigs are a useful starting point, but it is well worth tying your own to get things spot-on for your own preferences.

A Pole tip to float tip

The rig is attached with a simple loop knot. The distance between pole tip and float is important. The shorter it is, the closer control you have and the quicker you can hit bites with a quick lift. A sensible general optimum length is around 18" (45cm). If you are missing bites, try shortening the rig to make the gap smaller. If you are accidentally dragging the rig about or wind is interfering, a longer gap is sensible.

B Pole Float

The size and type of pole float you pick will vary according to conditions, but a good general rule is to use about 0.1g per foot of water. For a rig used to fish down the central track of a canal in 5ft of water, for example, a pole float carrying 0.5g of weight would be adequate. If conditions are rough, a heavier float tends to give better control so you might well scale up.

C Bulk or Spread shot

How you distribute shot has a critical effect on presentation. A number of small, evenly-spaced shot will give a slow fall of the bait, ideal for fishing 'on the drop' for fish like roach and rudd. For bigger fish, a bulk shot pattern (shot clustered together in one single 'bulk') is more useful, as pictured here, which will take the bait down quickly to the bottom. You'll get more positive bites by positioning a bulk of shot not too far off bottom – generally 14-16in (35-40cm) is fine.

D Hooklength and Final Shot

The final shot on our rig are of crucial importance. There are usually two smaller shot which could be down to a size 10 or 12. The very last shot is known as the 'tell tale' because it is this one that will move first when a fish takes the bait, telling us we have a bite. A common cause of missing bites is having this final shot too far from the hook. 3-4in (7-10cm) is sensible to start with, but if bites are really cagey, you could put this final tiny shot as close as 2in (4cm) to the hook. It is also commonplace to use a hooklength of line for the final few inches to the hook, attached loop to loop. Modern low diameter lines are ideal for this. However, for larger species such as tench and carp, many anglers prefer to fish 'straight through' with just one length of line for the whole rig to avoid the potential weak point of a knot. It's always good to have some spare hooklengths tied up. If you make a supply all the same length you can instantly switch, safe in the knowledge you are still at the exact same depth.

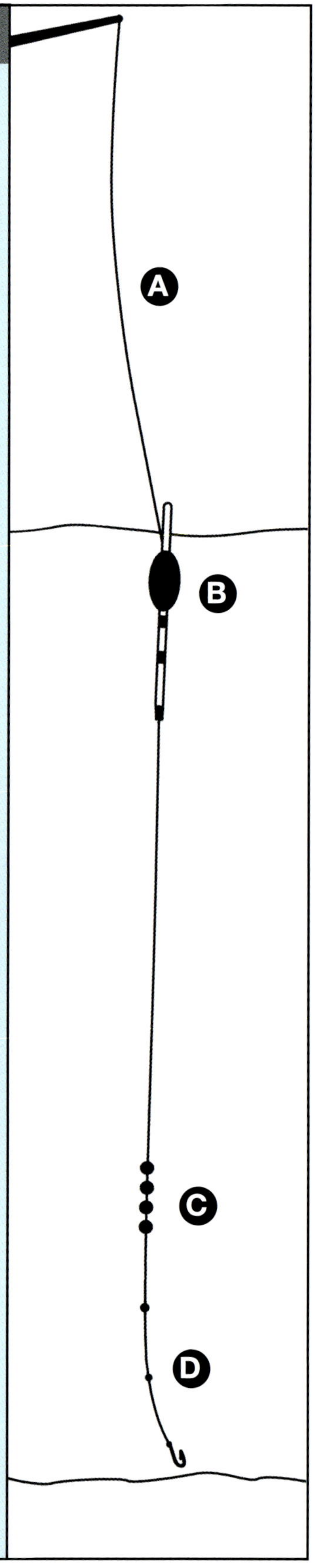

Pole Floats

For pure sensitivity, nothing beats a fine-bristled pole float for canal fishing. Various designs exist and all have their specific purposes.

Pole floats generally have three parts: a tip or 'bristle', a body and a stem. They are fixed in place by passing the line through a little wire eye and then two or three pieces of fine rubber tubing (sometimes called 'float sleeves' or 'float rubbers'), which should fit snugly to trap the line against the stem but not so tight that the float cannot be moved up or down with a little effort. It's best to have the final sleeve slightly overlapping the base of the stem, which helps prevent tangles.

If possible, it is best to have the float tip or 'bristle' set so that as little as possible is showing, although you may need some leeway for larger baits or dicey conditions.

The lower 'stem' of pole floats is made of either wire or carbon. Wire stems settle more quickly, but carbon versions seem kinder to your line and cause less kinking when you alter the depth.

Dibbers and shorter floats *(first and second from left)* are aimed for fishing close to the bank or features. They feature thicker tips that are ideal for bigger baits like worms or corn. Their small size make them unobtrusive in shallow swims. These are just the job for dropping a bait on the near or far bank of the canal, where quality fish might fancy a good mouthful.

Slim-Bodied pole floats *(middle two)* are delicate weapons for when you want a slow, even fall of your bait. These are spot on for presenting baits such as bread punch or pinkies, which roach will often take on the way down. They tend to feature a fine bristle and a light carbon stem. The

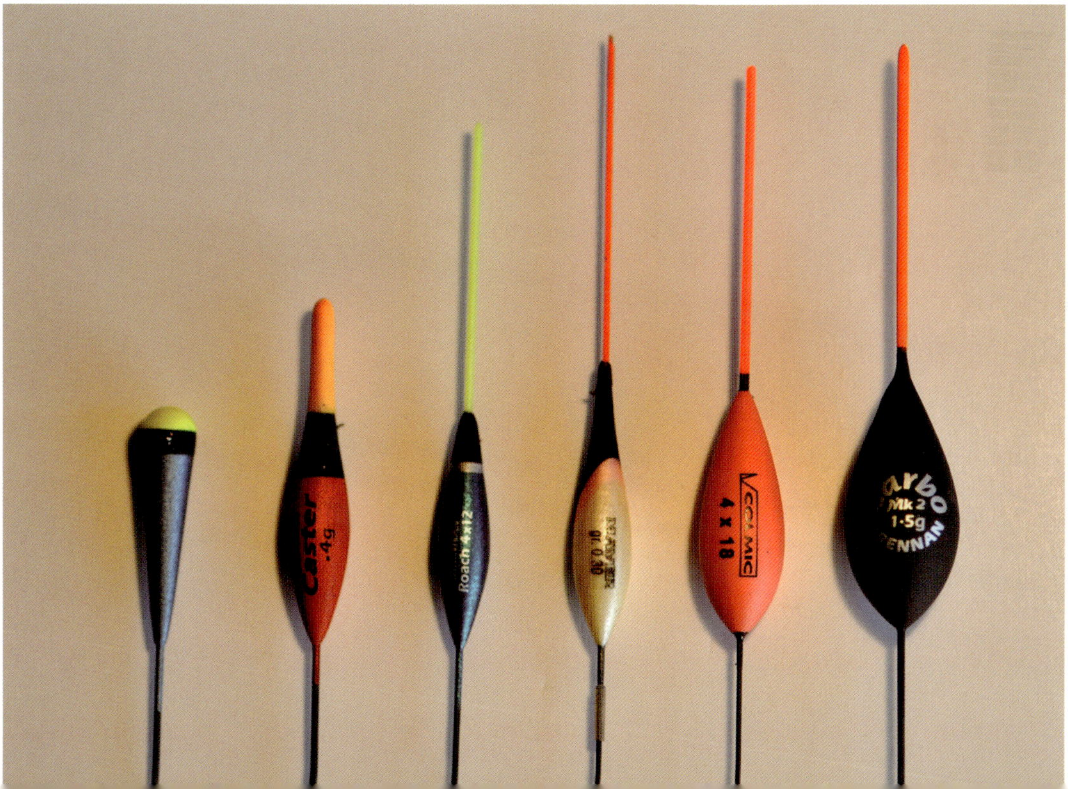

slender body will settle a little at a time as a series of small shots register. Bites on the drop are often signalled by the float tilting or stopping as this happens.

Pear-shaped/sturdy pole floats

(last two on the right, previous page) are for fishing on or near the bottom. These offer decent stability and are great all-rounders that help to keep your bait still on the deck. Those with chunkier bodies offer maximum steadiness, and the heaviest, long stemmed versions are perfect for deep water and ugly conditions.

Winders and Rig Storage

Pole rigs can be neatly stored on winders, which fit in purpose-made boxes. In this manner you can tie up a good selection for convenient storage. These can then be labelled with a permanent marker or sticker to denote line strength, rig type and hook size.

Accuracy is key on the canals – which makes the pole the natural weapon of choice for many towpath anglers.

FLOAT FISHING with RUNNING LINE

When it comes to catching fish on canals, there are many successful methods beyond the pole. Even if you do own a quality long pole, there are advantages to using a rod and reel from time to time. It allows you to sneak into tighter swims and avoid cluttering busy towpaths. You have fewer accessories and less fuss than a typical pole fishing session, making it easier to travel light and reach distant areas. Last but not least, the rod and reel approach is less likely to spook your quarry when the canal runs very clear and fish don't appreciate a pole tip waving over their heads.

For most canal fishing, the waggler is the most useful float. Attached bottom-end only, it is also easy to avoid floating debris and surface tow by putting the rod tip under the water and giving it a couple of pulls after you've cast out.

A few golden rules keep waggler fishing smooth and avoid hassle. The first is always to lock the float in place with at

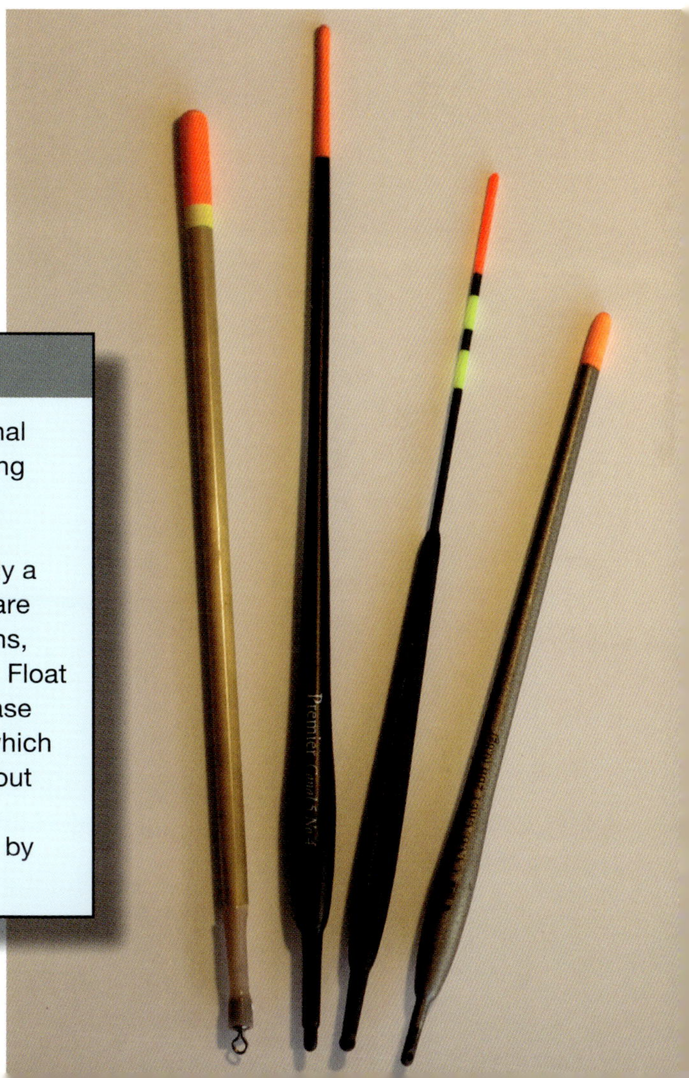

CANAL WAGGLERS

Fine-tipped insert wagglers or tapered 'canal specials' are ideal for canal fishing, providing sensitivity for shy biters such as roach and skimmers. These should always be dotted down as far as possible so you can see only a minimum of the bright tip. Thicker models are useful for larger baits and difficult conditions, whether made of modern materials or quill. Float adaptors are also a must (as seen at the base of the first float on the left on the picture) which allow you to change floats in seconds without breaking tackle down. I prefer the versions with swivels, which also help you hook fish by collapsing on the strike.

least two-thirds of the shot required to cock the float (so a waggler taking 3BB should have at least a weight of 2BB right by the base of the float). This helps to avoid tangles. The rest of the weight can be either 'strung' evenly to give a slow fall of the bait, or bulked together to reach the bottom quickly, with just a couple of much smaller shot between bulk and hook.

Another good rule is to select a float that you can cast comfortably to the distance required. If you have to force the cast, you're more likely to tangle or miscast. Sometimes a slightly larger float gives better control when there is breeze or tow on the water.

A quality reel line is a must for smooth casting. Modern lines have low diameters, making even a 4-5lb mono capable of sending out quite a delicate float. Tackle strength will vary according to species however. A 2½-3lb reel line would be adequate for roach and rudd, but for carp you might go as high as 10lb.

Rods are a trickier area for canals, since the market is now flooded with 'power' or carp models designed to fish overstocked puddles. These are fine for targeting big fish, but a far better tool for traditional canal species is a light match rod. A shorter model, down to as little as 10ft, can also be useful and I have even used light lure rods to fish a small waggler.

Presentation is Key

Perhaps the main disadvantage of waggler fishing compared to the pole is accuracy. If you can loose feed and cast to a tight area time and again, you will catch more fish. Picking a marker on the far bank to aim at is one solution, but practice makes perfect.

The waggler really comes into its own on shallow narrowboat canals; once the depth exceeds several feet it becomes less and less practical. The same could be said when conditions become blustery or the canal starts to flow harder. Presentation then becomes trickier. Sometimes you'll still catch 'on the drop' with baits such as bread or pinkies falling through

The waggler is a great method for canals, and with far less gear required than pole fishing you can change locations quicker if need be.

the water. But to get the bigger fish you must often alter things to keep your bait on the bottom. When it's hard to keep the bait still, you may need to set the float 'overdepth' – in other words, somewhat deeper than the swim. Removing a shot or two can help stop the float from dragging under. As with pole fishing, it is always a good idea to mark the depth carefully against the rod (usually with Tippex or by sticking the hook in the rod handle and counting the rings to the float).

Achieving control takes some practice, but the waggler can be a fun and highly skilful method. It certainly pays to be methodical and adapt to conditions: for example you might begin a session by catching fish at mid-depth, before trying overdepth for a better one.

Lots of small factors come into play. The splash of a float landing, for example, can be a curse or a blessing. Occasionally it might attract hungry fish; most of the time however, it's sensible to overcast slightly and draw the float gently into position to where you've been feeding.

Another good practice is to establish a rhythm of feeding and casting. If you regularly loose feed and then cast over it, you can trick the fish into thinking your bait is just another free offering. Bites can come at any time and the best waggler anglers hardly use a rest, preferring to hold the rod at all times.

You might not be able to lift and drop the bait like a pole angler, but little pulls and regular recasts earn extra bites, as does tinkering with the depth or casting just off the baited area to see if a bigger fish or two is keeping a slight distance. In essence, waggler fishing can be as active or as lazy as you make it.

Alternatives

It's also worth briefly mentioning different float methods, which can be just the ticket when the waggler is less than ideal. Very deep canals, or those with a steady flow are just two examples where you might need a plan B if you want to float fish with rod and reel.

A stick float can be highly effective on any waterway with a healthy flow to it, especially those venues which are essentially canalised rivers. Lock gates and side streams are other obvious spots to try tactics more regularly associated with rivers. Indeed, sometimes it is a mistake to try and keep your bait dead still where there is a flow. The bait you loose feed will be anything but static, so your hookbait must behave similarly.

Deep water also poses a challenge for float fishing. If the depth becomes anywhere near a rod length, casting becomes very difficult. The best solution is often to use a sliding float or 'slider'. These are large waggler-style floats with a swivel at the bottom. Rather than locking in place with shot, these floats cock upright by hitting a stop knot or float stop, which can be positioned as much as 12-15ft deep. All your shot can then be placed much nearer the hook, making casting much easier.

Quite a specialised method, but worth researching if your local Cut is very deep.

The spoils of an enjoyable session on the waggler, with caster-caught fish from both mid-water and on the bottom.

LURE FISHING

When it comes to catching pike, perch or any of the predatory species on canals, there are a lot of reasons to recommend lure fishing. In simple terms, it is an exciting way to search a lot of water. The tackle is light and can be relatively inexpensive, but it can also be extremely effective. A high proportion of my best canal pike and perch were caught on lures.

Perhaps what I like best about lure fishing is its great mobility. A rod, a net, a shoulder bag and you're away. You can set up and pack away in minutes, making a sneaky session before or after work an easy option. This lightness and flexibility also makes it a brilliant method for those who rely on public transport to go fishing.

In many ways, lure fishing is also an ideal method for canals. With long casting seldom called for, you can cover virtually all of the water, roaming the towpath in search of fish. And in a nutshell this process of cast and move is the essence of successful lure fishing. Predators are seldom spread out evenly and it is up to you to go and find them. Access points and open areas can get heavily fished and are also favoured by poachers. Travel light however and you can reach those interesting areas that are scarcely ever tried.

Seek and Destroy

Lure fishing on any canal is a case of trial and error, in terms of trying different artificials and locations. While you cannot guarantee the next fish that sees your lure will take it, by covering as many hungry mouths as possible you increase your odds hugely. Even on the worst of days, a lure that drops onto a predator's nose stands a chance of being hit, and in fact the only time you stand zero chance is when the water has frozen over.

The craft of finding the fish becomes much easier on a clear canal, or one full of features. Wherever you try there is an element of guesswork and covering the water. It can also involve a willingness to take some risks, since predators love snags and tight areas.

Keep in Touch!

Hits can come at any time when lure fishing, from the first seconds the lure hits the water to the very end of the cast. Always try to keep some tension and try to feel what the lure is doing. If it feels suspicious, strike!

Canals tend to demand accurate, short-range casting. Quite often this will be a case of a simple underarm swing or side casts and with practice you'll be able to drop your lure on a sixpence. Another useful skill is carefully checking or 'feathering' the line, by gently applying your index finger to the reel spool as the lure touches down. This helps accuracy and also saves your expensive lures from ending up in bushes and snags.

Any areas of cover or structure are worth exploring. Depth changes, such as where the bottom drops away around lock gates and marinas, are often key. Another crucial zone on canals is the 'shelf' on each side. All predators like the sloping sides of man-made channels. These are like corridors, the slope itself offering a degree of cover from which to patrol and attack. Two absolutely classic areas to get that bone-jarring hit are as the lure drops or dives down the far slope, and at the end of the cast, as the lure comes over the near slope over the head of a waiting attacker. Pike will often hit at the last second so never be in too much of a hurry to lift the lure clear of the water at the end of each cast.

Your retrieve itself can vary immensely: from a painfully slow 'death-warmed-up' speed with soft or jointed lures, right through to a fast, pulsating affair. Either way, it's worth remembering that every lure is different and every fishing day is different. With practice, you'll be able to get your lures working just as you like them. Little twitches and pauses create a 'stop-start' injured fish feel; sometimes a simple, steady retrieve works better.

THE RIGHT MOVES

With any lure, the key is in finding a 'taking' retrieve. In plain English that means working your artificial to give it an 'action' that brings you confidence and excites the fish. With any new lure, a good place to start is with a quick test in the margin by your feet.

Tackle for the Cut

The art of lure fishing might be quite a broad church, and just as canals vary, a range of set-ups can be used on different waters. Were I to pick just one outfit, however, I would take a light-to-medium lure or spinning rod capable of casting lures in the 10-30g category. Personally I also find longer rods advantageous too, as you get far better reach with a 9 or 10ft blank than you will with a shorter model. In overgrown or awkward spots, this extra reach can be invaluable.

Much heavier set-ups are sometimes favoured by pike anglers, but I find the mid-weight is much more fun with typical canal pike, which are not usually huge. That said, with 20-30lb braided line, such a set-up is more than capable of landing a large fish, and in fact two of my canal 20-pounders were landed on a mid-weight spinning rod.

A pleasant amble is generally involved when lure fishing, with the intention of exploring every corner.

Another fun option is to go with a lighter set-up, capable of casting lures as light as just two grams – indeed, this is the only way to do justice to the smallest of lures. For canals with a good head of perch, chub, small pike or zander, this is about as much fun as it gets. Whatever set-up you choose though, the most important thing is to pick a rod that suits your lure choices. Most rods have a cast rating in grams: a happy match will help you to 'feel' your artificials working properly.

Reel choices can also be varied. Some lure anglers like the feel of a multiplier or 'baitcaster' reel. These work very well with larger lures, but they do take some getting used to. Equally, I've never found them very useful with smaller artificials and for most canal anglers a decent fixed-spool reel will be all that is required.

When it comes to your line, there really is no contest between braid and mono. Braid is fine in diameter, exceptionally strong and with virtually no stretch you get a far superior 'feel' for your lures. 20-30lb braid is ideal for general use, or for ultra-light applications, braids of around 10lb cast superbly but are still strong.

Naturally, the other absolute essential on virtually every canal is a wire trace, plus spares. Even if pike are a rarity, you risk losing lures and killing fish by not using one. These consist of a swivel, 16in or so of wire and a snap link, which allows you to change lures in seconds.

Classic Lures

The lures themselves are a subject of fascination in their own right. You could spend a lifetime collecting them, such are the countless models available, but some lend themselves to canal fishing much better than others. Aside from the bigger ship canals, you will rarely find much need for artificials that sink or dive to vast depths.

Good old-fashioned favourites still have their place on the towpath. Spinners, with their deadly combination of pulse and flash, will always catch predatory fish, although line twist can be a problem, so where possible, I prefer to go for in-line models where the body stays constant as opposed to twisting the line. Spoons can be equally good and I've had a lot of pike on traditional models, which offer a seductive swerve and flash with a simple, steady turn of the reel. You can experiment with different sizes for these lures depending on species, but one deadly and underused trick for perch is to tip

Dominic's Tip

One advantage of single hook jigs is that they tend to avoid trouble with snags. If you do get snagged however, one handy trick is to 'ping' the lure free. This is done by keeping the line tight, pointing the rod at the snag and making a quick, firm pluck with a finger on the line *(see illustration)*. You might need to tighten or clamp down on the drag to do this. It takes a certain knack, but will often bounce your lure free. Walking a few yards to reverse the angle can also help to free snagged lures.

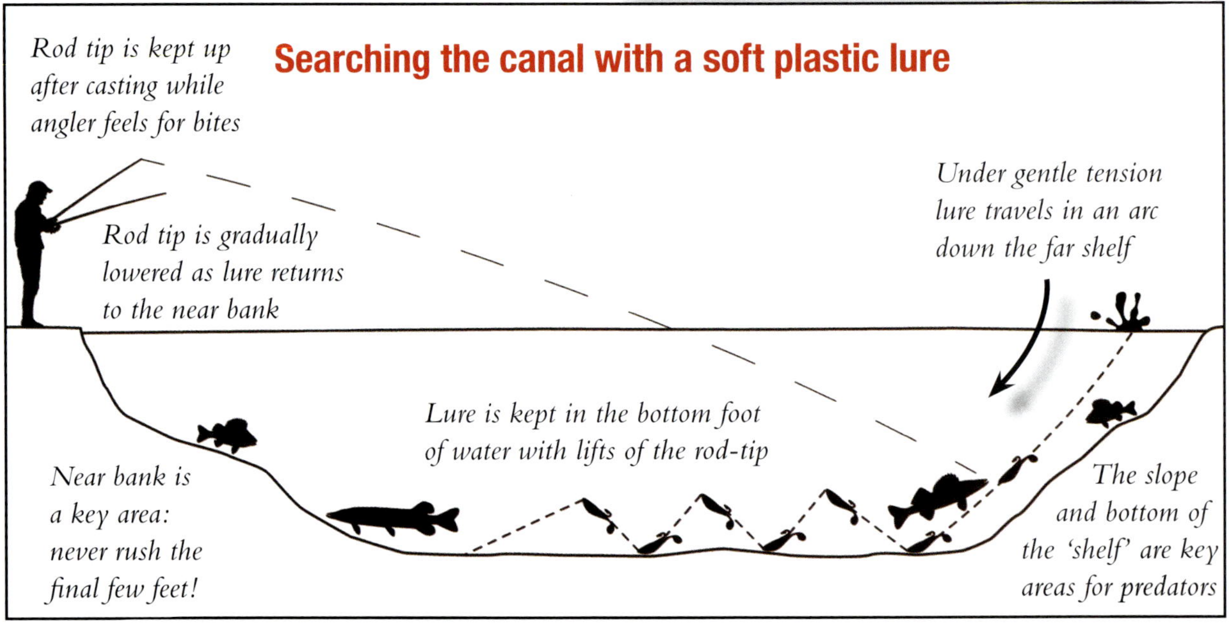

the hook with a worm, which is ideal for converting following fish into takers.

Plugs also retain a certain charm and effectiveness for canal fishing. Floating, shallow-diving plugs can be excellent on smaller canals especially. Cast tight to cover, or along the margins, these kick up a stir and are much loved by jack pike. I also have great faith in one or two variants of the standard, traditional wooden plug. Models with internal rattles are well worth a look if the water in your local Cut is seldom very clear. Jointed plugs are also great catchers and the modern, multi-sectioned versions are excellent. Quality jointed plugs are especially invaluable in winter, where their extra wiggle allows the angler to fish them more slowly if the pike are feeling cold and lethargic.

A small, single hook jig tempted this typical canal zander. These are brilliant, all-round lures.

DOES COLOUR MATTER?

While it is only one part of the puzzle, the colour of your lure can be an important consideration. Subtle, realistic-looking lures are the natural choice for clear water. Brighter hues cut through the murk however, and I also believe a large, loud offering can bring out the aggressive side of lethargic pike. Every rule can be broken, but it is up to you to find out what works on the day.

Soft Plastic Lures

Besides traditional models, a whole new generation of soft plastic lures is now available to the lure angler. These come in many guises, from ready-rigged versions to rubbery bodies you must thread onto a weighted hook (a 'jig head'). These have terrific movement in the water and it would be hard to fish many of them in the 'wrong' manner, although your technique can vary from a straight, steady turning of the reel to a much slower, closely controlled retrieve across the bottom for deep lying fish: a key method for perch and zander.

One really major plus point about modern soft plastic lures is that they are so incredibly versatile. Different weights can be used for different scenarios and depths: they work fast or slow, shallow or deep. I also like those with just a single hook. Not only do these snag less, they also do a lot less damage to the fish than trebles, which can tangle horribly in landing nets (for the sake of both the fish and my own sanity I tend to crush the barbs on all my treble hooks). They also tend to be cheap compared to traditional lures, making you less afraid to cast into those risky spots loved by predators.

The technique of fishing soft 'jig'-style offerings is quite different to presenting traditional lures. So often with species like zander and perch it is about keeping in close contact with the lure and keeping it in the bottom foot or so of water. The rod tip is kept higher than usual, often at head height (the opposite to spinning or plug fishing, where you might typically lower the tip to avoid bringing your artificial too high in the water). A common way to fish for perch, and especially zander, is to retrieve quite slowly, with turns of the reel and small twitches on the rod tip causing the jig to lift and fall. At no point does the line go slack: a little tension is always maintained and any pluck of interest met with an upward strike. Zander in particular can give quite gentle takes.

A particularly deadly trick with a soft plastic lure is to cast to the far side and 'feel' it down. Held under a little tension it will flutter down the far shelf in an attractive arc *(see diagram page 146)*. 'On the drop' takes are not always obvious, especially from zander. If the fish moves directly towards the angler all you might detect is a sudden slackening of tension; anything suspicious should be met with a strike.

LURE ESSENTIALS

How light can you travel? As tempting as it is to leave all but a rod behind, some requisites must always be with you. Among these are a pair of sturdy, long forceps or long-nosed pliers and an unhooking mat (some mats can be rolled around a net or carried on your back).

Dominic's Tip

A good tip with any floating lure is to pause once you have cast out. Pike are instinctively curious, and by counting to five or ten before you start to reel in you are giving any nearby murderers the chance to home in on your artificial and get within striking distance.

Above: Norbert Darby cradles a lure-caught pike of 12lbs.

Jigging and Drop Shotting at Close Quarters

Takes can come anywhere in a canal when you are lure fishing. Most anglers tend to eye up the far bank first, but in many cases fish can also be found sitting right under the rod tip on the near side. This is especially true around walls, lock gates and along boats, and another advantage of soft plastic jigs is that they can be fished vertically, up and down on the spot if necessary. On coloured canals you can even walk slowly along the towpath, working a lure under the rod tip as you go.

Drop shotting adds an extra degree of finesse to the practice of 'vertical' fishing. It involves a separate weight, much like a small leger bomb, that sinks to the bottom while one or more small, soft plastic lures are suspended above at right angles to the line. As the weight is separate, this allows you to fish very small artificials with a great deal of subtlety. Sensitive rods are used to make tiny movements to manipulate the lures, which tend to be worked right under the rod tip, or cast short distances. It can be an excellent method for perch and zander on canals, perfect for searching structures and the sides of boats and moorings really thoroughly.

Drop shotting set-ups are deadly for close-range fishing around likely features.

Lure angler Andy Mytton searches along a walled canal bank right under the rod tip. Moments later a small zander snatched his rubber shad.

The Chase is On

The colder months might still be favoured by traditionalists, but with no closed season in many cases, lure fishing can be carried out year-round on canals. Warmer water and more weed growth carry their own challenge and call for a different arsenal.

Modern lures such as spinner baits and weedless plastic lures are one great answer to overgrown canals or poor visibility. Spinner baits provide both a strong pulse

Urban spots can also be highly productive: try heavy braid or single hook lures to negotiate snags.

and some snag resistance, allowing you to cast right into those hairy spots where pike lie in wait.

As a general rule, predators will be higher in the water from spring onwards. On some rustic, neglected canals you might find 3ft of depth choked in weed and just 1ft of water above it. Successful fishing is all about presenting lures in the upper layers and casting accurately into little clear patches. Floating lures now come to the fore, as well as slow sinkers or those described as 'suspending'.

Perhaps the most exciting of all the options in spring and summer fishing is to go for a floating lure that will splash, pop and wiggle its way across the surface. Such artificial baits are a breed apart. Classic surface plugs come with scooped fronts, or even paddles and propellers to create disturbance and draw in predators. These are your choice for open water or gaps in the weed. But sometimes even more useful are weedless floating frogs, mice and other oddities that can be skipped, hopped and twitched right through lilies, duck weed and the swampy areas pike love. Some can be bought but I have had excellent fun making my own floating mice and ducklings in the past. In fact my best lure-caught canal pike, a 17-pounder, took a mouse made of balsa and deer hair!

Takes can be incredibly dramatic, with the water exploding and fish vaulting clear. Such attacks on the surface can be harder to connect with, but if you can hold your nerve, it's often worth waiting just a split second longer to let the fish engulf the target properly.

Summer fishing does come with a little health warning, however. Pike, especially, are fragile in warm water. They thrash hard even once you get them on the bank and demand careful handling, with an absolute minimum time spent out of the water. It's your call, but having seen pike die in hot weather shortly after release, I will no longer fish for them in such conditions.

Seb Nowosiad is a picture of concentration as he brings a soft jig to life.

John Cheyne jigs for zander on the Grand Union: note the high angle of the rod tip.

Get stuck in!

Watch eight out of ten anglers on a canal and you'll see the same pattern emerge: they always stop at the open swims or 'pegs' but leave the bushy parts out. In doing so, they are missing out a great deal of likely water – and pike love inaccessible, snaggy areas. For the lure angler it is a question of responsibility; you must never cast from a position where it is impossible to land a fish. But where possible, get stuck in. If you take no risks, you get fewer chances.

I caught this cracking perch from a deep canal basin. The area was full of fingerling roach – so my offering of a silver shad was accepted immediately.

My Favourite Canal Lures

TOP ROW *(left to right)*:

Savage Gear Four-Play: A modern, multi-jointed plug. Excellent for pike.
Jointed Rapala: A classic plug with added wiggle, ideal for shallow canals.

SECOND ROW *(left to right)*:

Shakespeare Big S: A plug with bulky presence and added rattle.
Rapala Shad Rap: A smaller traditional bait, for zander and perch as well as pike.
Storm Suspending Shad: Terrific for weedy waters, will fish slowly and 'hang' in fishy gaps.

THIRD ROW *(left to right)*:
Two **In-line spinners**, good for all predators with a steady retrieve.
Kuusamo Professor: An excellent spoon for big pike.

FOURTH ROW *(left to right)*:

A trio of soft plastic lures mounted on jig heads: Two **Kopyto Shads** (3in and 2½in) and **Curly Tail Grub**, superb for zander, jacks, perch and chub.

FIFTH ROW *(left to right)*:

Spinner Bait: Weird-looking, but creates a strong pulse and excellent snag resistance for weedy water.
Weedless Frog: An exciting option for pike hiding by lily pads and duck weed.
Rapala Skitterpop: A hell-raiser for spring surface fishing.

THE CANALS OF BRITAIN

An Angler's Guide

Britain's canals represent an incredible and varied fishing resource. We encounter bottomless ship channels and tiny little affairs; gritty, urban waterways and neglected backwaters. While all canals have similarities, every one is unique. My own journey has been an undertaking of blood, silt and tears, not to mention endless emails, phone calls and miles on the road, but utterly fascinating.

An exhaustive study of the nation's many hundreds of miles of canal would take several books. Nevertheless, our aim here is to guide you through all of the major waterways, as well as a healthy selection of those smaller, less celebrated places. We cannot hope to cover every venue or mile of water, but every part of Britain is included here, from the Scottish Highlands down to sunny Cornwall and everywhere else in between.

Someone also suggested that we include a couple of entirely fictional canals, just to see if readers would spot them. While it might have been tempting to include the 'Guernsey Union' or the 'Penzance Imperial', a look through the waters of reality reveals more than enough surprise and intrigue to keep the canal enthusiast busy for a lifetime. Furthermore, I found many of the most prolific and interesting of all the canals to be the least fished.

As well as issues like licences and fishing clubs, our aim is also to bring you some of the juicy facts and figures for Britain's canals. These include strange trivia, snippets of history and of course notable captures from each venue (all weights are in pounds and ounces). What I cannot do is give you every swim and secret – and besides, where would the fun be in that? Part of the joy of canal fishing remains its mystery, and that special pleasure in discovering your own hot spots and areas of note.

All information presented here is accurate at the time of publication. You'll also notice that some of the really major canals have more than one entry, as they stretch between different regions (for example the Trent and Mersey Canal could be classed as both a Midlands and northern venue) and in these cases we deal with these waters with specific regional information.

Tackle shops and fishing clubs do of course change, as does the proliferation of species in any given water. We have not included waters such as drains and dykes here either, which are not, strictly speaking, canals, although a lot of the tactics for canal fishing could be said to apply to these waters too.

On many of Britain's canals, tickets can be bought 'on the bank'. However, as a general rule we would advise that you seek out a local tackle shop first- which are always a great source of up-to-date information on how the canals are fishing.

SOUTH-WEST ENGLAND

The canals of the West Country may not be incredibly numerous, but what they lack in quantity they more than make up for in quality. Rural waterways feature prominently, including some of the most beautiful you could wish for. The clearer waters certainly make for some fantastic sight fishing opportunities, with stalking methods and fly fishing excellent fun. Perhaps it is ironic that holiday anglers head for busy commercial fisheries and coastlines when a good handful of absolutely stunning canals offer excellent value mixed fishing open to all.

Bude Canal *

Main species: Roach, rudd, bream, tench, carp, eels, perch, gudgeon, flounder, trout
Notable catches: Bream 7.06, Carp 26.00, Perch 3.12, Roach 1.12
Match record: 84lbs (bream and carp)

The Bude Canal represents the final 'Cut' of any description as you travel to the far south west. For the visiting angler, the first 1½ miles are fishable and offer good variety. In the wide sections, bream and silver fish are present in good numbers, while stocked carp are also common from 2-pounders to much larger fish.

Perhaps the weirdest and most unique aspect of fishing the Bude Canal is the prospect of a jaw-dropping surprise catch. Trout are fairly widespread, along with flounders and even the occasional school bass, making this a wonderfully unpredictable fishery and a fine stop-off for the visiting angler. It can get busy with boats and walkers in the summer, hence an early start is highly recommended.

Recommended areas: Try the wide section, just off The Crescent, where you'll also find a handy car park. Take a walk out of town for more traditional, feature-filled swims and less human traffic.

Disabled access: Flat bankside and swims by The Crescent are ideal.
Angling clubs/Permit details: Bude Canal AA (www.budecanalangling.co.uk). Full membership is only for locals, but day tickets are available from the Post Office, The Crescent, Bude EX23 8LE (01288 352048)

Exeter Ship Canal *

Main species: Roach, rudd, bream, tench, carp, perch, pike

Notable catches: Carp 42.03, Perch 4.02, Pike 32.04, Bream 10.04
Match record: 38lbs (bream)

Built in the 1560s to dodge the highly taxed River Exe, the Exeter Canal stands as one of the earliest and most historic of man-made channels. Built for ocean-going vessels, it is a beast of a waterway with weedy depths typically to 12ft down the middle.

From spring to autumn, fishing for bream and tench can be excellent on pole or feeder tactics. Roach, rudd and perch also feature. An atypical canal in several respects, many regulars see it as a big fish water. It can be a tough nut to crack, but at one time produced both the carp and pike UK canal records to local angler Pete Gregory.

A surreal mid-winter scene on the Exeter Ship Canal. In the background you can see the city's historic cathedral.

Dave Sellick took this solid canal bream on the pole, targetting the main track with dead maggots.

Recommended areas:
Lime Kilns: For all species, but a favourite haunt for pike and carp especially.
Topsham Strait: (follow the track past *The Swans Nest* pub) for skimmers, bream and tench.
Countess Wier Swing Bridge/Clapperbrook/Double Locks: are usually less busy but also have their share of fish. Some good bream, perch and carp.

Trivia

The Exeter Canal features Britain's oldest working lock gates, made in 1567.

Angling clubs/Tackle shops/Permits:
Exeter AA (www.exeterangling association.co.uk). Tickets from Exeter Angling Centre, Smythen St, Exeter EX1 1BN (01392 436404)

Don't miss: The *Double Locks Inn* and *Turf Locks* are great places to sample local tipples when the fishing is slow. Mine's a pint of Dartmoor Jail Ale.

If you are prepared to walk you can find really secluded spots on the Exeter Ship Canal.

Grand Western Canal *

Main species: Roach, rudd, tench, bream, perch, pike

Notable catches: Rudd 2.05, Roach 1.11, Carp 24.00, Bream 8.02

Match record: 55.04lbs (mostly tench) Dave Pullman

Names are deceptive things and this canal, better known as the Tiverton or 'Tivvy' Canal, is 'Grand' in terms of beauty rather than size. With weedy, often aquarium clear water it is one of my favourite places on the planet. There is a good reason you're likely to spot a kingfisher here: it's alive with fish. And while you won't find many monsters, there are some cracking tench, roach and rudd. Pole fishing is the perfect way to get bites. Summer fishing is excellent using corn or casters, while bread punch works well for winter roach and bream. There are also many jack pike, which provide plenty of fun on lure tackle.

In my eyes, this is also one of the best flyfishing waters in the West Country. Summer roach and rudd readily take small wets and dries, while in the winter the local predators love striking at pike flies.

Recommended areas: Try the town end (near Canal Hill) for bream, roach and the occasional big carp. Sellick Bay/ Greenway at Halberton is the renowned tench area. Many other spots are also worth investigating. Be prepared to travel light with polarising glasses.

Disabled access: A wheelchair-friendly platform exists just off the bridge at Greenway.

Sunrise on Bridgwater Docks. Local killjoys have recently rendered some swims 'no fishing' zones. But the quieter spots still hold stacks of fish.

This handsome devil of a grass snake was sunning itself on the towpath. Later on it slithered into a tackle bag for a snooze.

An incredible bream of 8.02lb for Russ Hilton. Corn or casters single out some excellent fish on the 'Tivvy'.

Trivia

The exceptionally beautiful water lilies of the Grand Western Canal were once cultivated by traders to be sold on to ornamental gardens.

Angling clubs/Tackle shops & Permits: Tiverton AA is the local club, season and day permits available from Cullompton Coarse & Carp EX15 1BW (01884 839273) just off the M5, or in Tiverton itself Exe Valley Angling EX16 5DQ (01884 242275)

Taunton to Bridgwater Canal *

Main species: Roach, silver bream, bleak, rudd, perch, bream, tench, pike, chub
Notable catches: Pike 27.04, perch 2.08, Carp 26.00, chub 3.12
Match record: 81lbs (tench), Simon Garbutt, December 2013. A phenomenally varied list of species populate this waterway, which cuts through some beautiful scenery on the edge of the Somerset Levels. Once a nationally regarded match water, the roach fishing can still be excellent on bread or caster, while tench and bream are present in good numbers. Roving anglers catch plenty of pike too, with lures and flies working well in the shallow water. Perhaps the biggest surprise is the chub, however. Stocked several years ago, many of these fish have reached 2-3lb and love to haunt bridges and weed rafts in the more secluded sections. Carp also feature, although this canal is known for quality rather than quantity.

Recommended areas: Creech St Michael, Charlton and North Newton (Taunton AA) for roach, rudd, pike and tench.

Pike await the roving angler.

Bite-a-chuck sport can be had right through the winter, as Russ Hilton shows with his bag of rudd, roach and silver bream. Bread punch was the killer bait.

First class viewing: the West Country canals boast great conditions for fish-spotting. Here, a shoal of juvenile perch glides into view.

The wide waters near the *Boat and Anchor* pub (Bridgwater AA) are excellent for a mixed bag on pole or feeder. The Bridgwater end, including the docks, is very urban in places, but has some fine tench and perch.

Disabled access: Several priority fishing platforms to be found along the towpath from the *Boat and Anchor* pub, walking away from the motorway bridge.

Angling clubs/Tackle shops/Permits: Fishing rights are divided between two clubs, Taunton AA (www.taunton-angling.co.uk) and Bridgwater AA (www.bridgwaterangling.co.uk) with the dividing line at Higher Maunsell Lock. Try Somerset Angling, Bridgwater TA4 6PL (01278 431777) or Taunton Angling Centre TA1 1PA (01823 282518). Taunton AA permits are also available online.

.........Trivia.........

The Chard Canal was possibly Britain's shortest lived, surviving just 26 years from its opening in 1842 to closure in 1868.

Ilminster Canal
(formerly Chard Canal)

Main species: Roach, bream, perch, tench, carp

Notable catches: Carp 24.00, Roach 2.01

A mere 150 yards exist of this channel, once part of the Chard Canal, which was a commercial failure. Nevertheless, those few surviving yards are well stocked by the local fishing club, who hold regular friendly matches.

Angling clubs/Tackle shops/Permits: Ilminster AA (www.ilminsteraa.co.uk).

Recommended locations: Parking is at Canal Way, at the bottom of the recreation ground. The fishing is consistent throughout, pole or waggler-fished baits such as maggot, worm and pellet score best.

SOUTHERN ENGLAND AND LONDON

IN a sense the waterways of the Greater London area and the south illustrate perfectly the value of canals at the more crowded end of Britain. Even in central London, there is intriguing fishing to be found and an incredible list of species from the traditional to the accidental. In terms of specimen fishing there is also a cracking variety on offer, with some phenomenal untapped potential for large carp, tench, perch and other species across various waterways, and all at a fraction of the cost of the south's more exclusive stillwaters. For our purposes, our 'South' section begins in Milton Keynes and covers south of that.

The author enjoys a pole fishing session on the 'Basie' as the camera rolls. The film can be seen on YouTube.

Basingstoke Canal *

Main species: Roach, perch, bream, tench, carp

Notable catches: Bream 8.04, Carp 29.12, Tench 8.04, Perch 3.07, Pike 28.04

Match record: 57.10lbs, Reading Road Bridge 2010 (taken in winter!)

The 'Basie' as it is affectionately known to locals, is an excellent mixed fishery not to mention a historic waterway. Dug out for the purpose of shipping goods and supplies from Basingstoke to the Thames in London, parts of this once busy channel then fell into disrepair after the demise of canals. By the mid-1960s the canal was virtually derelict in places, with whole sections left dry and desolate, before locals fought back to save their beloved Cut.

A pretty place it can be too, with a real mixture of fishing. Sport on the whip or pole can be bite-a-chuck with baits such as bread punch or pinkie; alternatively, there are big perch, tench and even specimen carp if you know where to look. Unfortunately there are also hordes of crayfish, so durable baits and regular recasts make sense for the angler. Do please note that the closed season applies on this water.

This classic Cut also features in a special short film featuring the author. *Canal Fishing with Dominic Garnett* can be found on YouTube.

Like so many southern canals, the Basingstoke is absolutely teeming with fish.

Recommended locations:
Church Crookham, Hants (Basingstoke Canal AA): Plenty of roach and skimmers. The wide section at Poulters Bridge also has tench.
Bottom Flash, Aldershot (Basingstoke Canal AA): A huge wide section over 120ft across, this is a natural holding area for roach, bream and some huge carp. Pole and feeder work best, or boilie tactics for carp.
Disabled Access: Colt Hill Bridge (Odiham) has three purpose-made fishing stations.
Angling clubs/Tackle shops & Permits: Basingstoke Canal Angling Association (www.basingstokecanalaa.co.uk) is a well-run club with an excellent website detailing more on this great southern canal.
The Creel, Aldershot (01252 320871)

Don't miss: *The Fox and Hounds* pub (GU51 5NP) is a classic, canalside boozer. The fishing just a stone's throw away is decent too. The Basingstoke Canal Centre in Mytchett (GU16 6DD) is another good stop-off point with historic interest, activities for the kids and also sells fishing permits.

Chelmer & Blackwater Canal

Main species: Roach, perch, bream, pike, carp

Miles of under-fished canal make up this waterway, with some big surprises present for the roving specialist, including carp to over 30lbs. Please note that this water is subject to the CLOSED SEASON.

Recommended areas:
Hoe Mill/Papermill Lock/Heybridge Basin (Maldon AS): Consistent spots for pole and waggler fishing.
Angling clubs/Tackle shops/Permits:
Maldon AS (www.maldonas.co.uk),
JP Tackle, Maldon, CM9 5BS (01621 854588)

Chichester Canal

Main species: Roach, rudd, perch, bream, tench, gudgeon, eels, pike, carp, crucians

A very pretty canal of over four miles, there is a staggering range of species here, including some real specimens as well as traditional favourites. Carp are reputed to grow to over 30lbs, but the most eye-opening story from past times is that of an enormous pike witnessed by many anglers. It went uncaught for several years, before it is rumoured a local angler caught it at just over 40lbs in weight!

Recommended areas:
Canal Wharf: A likely bet for bream and carp, but angling only permitted from October to March.
Angling Clubs/Tackle shops & Permits: Chichester Canal Trust (01243 771262) runs the fishing. Day tickets available on the bank from the bailiff.
Also see: www.chichestercanal.org.uk

Grand Union Canal *

Main species: Roach, bream, tench, perch, gudgeon, carp

Notable catches: Chub 6.00, Rudd 2.02, Carp 46.04, Perch 4.04

This mighty canal is of such a great length, it could be thought of as the 'local Cut' by Southern and London anglers as well as Midlanders, hence our two entries for the Grand Union. Some of the prettiest stretches of all are found north of London in areas such as Leighton Buzzard and Aylesbury, the latter having its own branch of the canal. But there is also fishing to be had right in the capital on the Paddington Arm.

It can be hard to separate rumour from solid fact sometimes on such a vast water, but the Grand Union is well-known as a canal where monster fish can and do turn up. Chub to 6lb, have been caught here, to say nothing of the quality mixed fishing for traditional species. Perhaps the only major canal fish that doesn't appear to thrive is the pike.

Don't always expect traditional tactics to dominate here. The Grand Union has a bigger head of carp (including the current canal record) for example, than

..........Trivia..........

In 1983, 77-year-old angler Alfred Burtoo and his dog Tiny were surprised by the sight of a flying disc by the Basingstoke Canal. Burtoo then claims he was accosted by a group of small humanoid figures who took him to their UFO and examined him (poor old Alfred was too startled and polite to ask any questions such as 'Why do you breathe through your armpits?' or 'Have you seen any tench?'). Luckily for him, the martians considered him too old and weak for their purposes. But if you suspect Burtoo had been drinking, military police also claimed to have seen such a craft the same night.

Gudgeon fanatic Neil Williams plays a 'nuisance' bream!

The Grand Union is probably the UK's best canal for carp

Pike are not always prolific on the Grand Union – but the perch fishing can be outstanding, as Dan Sales demonstrates with a lure-caught specimen.

any other canal in the UK. They can turn up anywhere, but noted stretches contain concentrations of literally hundreds of these fish. Stepped up match or specimen tactics both have their place – and you're often as likely to see pellets and boilies in use as the traditional corn and worms.

Recommended areas:
Aylesbury Arm, Wilton (Tring Anglers): Excellent for bonus fish including bream, chub, perch and large roach. Try caster, worm and hemp.
Mill Road, Manor Fields (Milton Keynes AA): Good nets of bream and roach.
The Black Horse Inn (Milton Keynes AA): A good stretch to pole fish, with plenty of skimmers and perch.
Hemel Hempstead (London AA): Try Boxmoor for bream on feeder and pole.
Leighton Buzzard (Luton AC): A noted spot for carp. Try strong pole or specimen tackle close to boats for fish to double figures.
Paddington Arm (Waterway Wanderers): Try the wide sections near *The Black Horse* pub for bream, or Horsenden Lane for roach and perch to pinkies.
West Drayton (Waterway Wanderers): North of West Drayton Railway Station is a decent spot for float fishing, with roach and perch common.

Angling clubs/Tackle shops & Permits:
Aylesbury Angling Centre (01296 437555)
Milton Keynes Angling Centre (01908 374400)
Luton AC: www.lutonanglingclub.co.uk
Tring Anglers: www.tringanglers.org.uk
Blenheim AS: www.blenheimas.co.uk
London AA: www.londonanglers.net)
Waterway Wanderers Scheme(canalrivertrust.org.uk)

Hertford Union Canal

Main species: Roach, perch, pike
Notable catches: Pike 16.00

A short stretch of canal that connects the Lee Navigation to the Regent's Canal, this mile or so of water is worth a look for its roach shoals, odd perch as well as pike in the winter. A walk with lures is the best way to find them.

Angling clubs/Tackle shops/Permits:
Waterway Wanderers Scheme

Kennet and Avon Canal *

Main species: Roach, perch, bream, tench, bleak, barbel, pike
Notable catches: Chub 6.15, Perch 3.10, Carp 41.00
Match record: 53lbs (Bream and carp)

Another beast of a canal, the Kennet and Avon has a little something for just about anyone with fishing in their blood. In terms of classic pole fishing there are both traditional smaller species, but also some incredible surprises. Not least of all are the chub, making their way in from the Kennet, which run to over 6lb.

Specimen hunters in the know have long realised the potential of the canal for such unlikely monsters, although it can be very much a case of legwork and knowing your areas. Carp are also a feature on the canal. So are the perch that, like the chub, have grown huge on an endless supply of bleak and crayfish.

My own experience of the canal has been mostly lure fishing in the autumn and winter, which can be excellent fun. Covering the water with smaller lures such as jigs and spinners works well for jack pike as well as some terrific perch and chub.

NB: Other than sections such as the 'true canal' at Froxfield, many parts of this water are subject to the CLOSED SEASON.

Recommended areas:

Devizes (Devizes AA): Try the pounds slap bang in town for mixed nets and bonus tench and bream.

A deep bend in the rod here could mean anything from a double figure carp to a specimen chub.

Roving tactics work well for the perch, as Will Barnard demonstrates with a fantastic canal fish.

Foxhanger, Caen Hill (Devizes AA): Good nets of skimmers, plus bonus carp.
Seend to Semington (Devizes AA): Worth a try for tench and carp into double figures.
Great Bedwyn (Marlborough DAA): Decent area for pole fishing, with roach, perch and bonus bream.
The Salmon Cut (Reading DAA): A good stretch to try stepped-up pole gear or small lures for big perch and chub.
Froxfield (Reading DAA): Fantastic winter roach sport; try bread punch.
Midgham (Reading DAA): Worth a try for pike and carp, this also has a stream inlet where the canal species hunter has a good chance of adding barbel to his list!
Bathampton, Somerset (Bathampton AA): Decent roach fishing with hemp and caster.
Pewsey Wharf (Pewsey AC): A noted area for perch on lures or chopped worm tactics.

Angling clubs/Tackle shops/Permits: Devizes AA (www.devizesaa.org.uk), Bernie's Tackle, Devizes (01380 730712), Reading DAA (www.rdaa.co.uk) tickets from Reading Angling Centre, RG2 7PS (01189 872216)
Marlborough DAA (www.mdaa.co.uk)
Pewsey AC (www.pewseyfishingclub.com)

Trivia

Seen as a defensive line in World War Two, numerous 'pillbox'-style defensive positions can still be found along the Kennet and Avon Canal. For locations of these, try **www.derelictplaces.co.uk**

Lee Navigation *

Main species: Roach, bream, perch, tench, carp, pike

Notable catches: Carp 40.01, Perch 4.01, Pike 30.04, Tench 8.04

Once noted as a fine roach fishing water, the Lee Navigation is now rightly regarded as a 'big fish' water. Bream are well-established, with double-figure fish possible. Carp and perch too are present to an impressive size on this waterway which, strictly speaking, is a canalised river (there is generally a slow-moving flow). Nevertheless, it is arguably the best canalised waterway in the Greater London area, running right past the Olympic Stadium.

Do carp get any better-looking than this specimen common, caught by Dan Sales?

Perhaps the only sadness is that crayfish and cormorants have damaged parts of this waterway, but with the efforts of the Lee Anglers' Consortium and Canal and Rivers Trust, things are improving. Fish refuges have been set up to help to protect juvenile stocks and projects are on-going.

Recommended areas:
Enfield Lock (Lee AC): Good for mixed sport year-round, also some tench and large carp.
Stanstead Abbotts (Lee AC): Worth a try for decent perch, especially.
Ramney Lock Cut (Lee AC): Noted for good bream

Angling clubs/Tackle shops & Permits: Lee Anglers' Consortium (www.lee-anglers-consortium.co.uk), Try Lee Valley Tackle, E4 8AJ (020 8529 5444) or JB's Fishing Tackle, N9 8AH (020 8805 6050)

Don't miss: The *Fish and Eels* (EN11 0AY) is a suitably-titled pub right by the Lee Navigation where a weary angler might celebrate or commiserate with a decent pint of ale.

Trivia

There is evidence that the River Lea was altered as early as 1190 to make it more navigable: Incidentally the 'true' river still bears the name 'Lea', while the canalised parts are referred to as 'Lee'.

Casting into the unknown: The Lee Navigation offers a lot of underfished water.

Regent's Canal, London
(& Paddington Branch) *

Main species: Roach, bream, ruffe, perch, carp
Notable catches: Carp 23.00, roach 2.01

For those who don't mind the busy setting, this Cut in the heart of the capital offers challenging but rewarding mixed fishing. Parking can be an issue, but public transport is a reliable option, provided you travel light. An excellent starting point would be a fine-tipped waggler or whip, with relatively fine tackle and little and often feeding to contact roach and skimmers. The water in London's canals has never been clearer, which is why punched bread tends to be a must-have bait for silver fish. This clarity can make the fish really hug the features and sheltered areas. If you're really struggling, fishing with the worm under boats brings the occasional welcome perch. Generally, the fishing improves when boats pass and colour the water, making the fish feel safer. Extra bonus points if you can catch a ruffe!

A good head of carp to well over 20lbs are also present for the dedicated specimen hunter. Jack pike and perch are also caught if you rove with lures. A word of warning however: debris, such as the

Carp in central London? For the dedicated, there are some tough, wily fish to be found.

ubiquitous shopping trolley, can be rife, hence cheap, single-hook lures such as jigs are recommended. The towpath is generally safe these days, but do take a friend if you plan to fish in the evening.

Recommended areas:
Little Venice: A great holding area for large carp, as well as odd perch and silver fish. Behind Kings Cross: the canal opens out and can be worth a cast for bream and pike. Camden: is also worth a try for mixed bags. Try punched bread and chopped worm, fishing tight to barges if the fish are finicky.
Near London Zoo: Try maggot and groundbait for mixed nets. Fishes well in the summer when boats add some colour.

Disabled access: The canal is a busy place, but access is reasonable near Paddington station, where the main bridge over the canal also has ramps.

Angling clubs/Tackle shops & Permits:
Waterway Wanderers scheme/Free Fishing. Try www.londonangler.com for more info and catch reports.

Don't miss: For history buffs, the London Canal Museum is well worth a visit (12-13 New Wharf Rd, N1 9RT) www.canalmuseum.org.uk

Trivia

In 2012, Londoners were shocked to hear of the discovery of murdered Eastenders actress Gemma McCluskie in the Regent's Canal.

Casting into the Capital: a day on the Regent's Canal.

An 1800s view of Little Venice, London.

The Long Water Hampton Court

Main species: Roach, tench, carp
Notable catches: Mirror carp 32lbs

Developed in 1662 by none other than King Charles II, this stately canal is hardly an industrial era channel, but a show of wealth and power. Expect a healthy walk, but some fine tench and carp in distinguished surroundings once you get there.

Angling clubs & Permits: For day and season tickets, contact Hampton Court Palace (www.hrp.org.uk/Hampton-CourtPalace)

Trivia

The Oxford Canal is now a popular site for 'Geocaching'- a hobby like a high tech version of Letterboxing, where ramblers use GPS to find secret containers with hidden logbooks (or at least that's what I think that rustling in the bushes was).

Oxford Canal

(see also Midlands)

Main Species: Roach, bream, perch, gudgeon, chub, carp, pike
Notable Catches: Chub 5.06, Roach 1.08
Match record: 84.10lbs (chub)

Another waterway that could be considered both a southern and a Midlands canal, stretching 78 miles and connecting Oxford with the River Thames, as well as the Grand Union and Coventry Canals. It has some beautiful stretches too, making it a popular route with boats and walkers. For the angler, stocks are as varied as they've ever been. Some huge catches of chub have won matches in recent years, while rumours persist of carp that would smash the current canal record.

Recommended Areas:
Enslow Wharf, Bletchingdon (Littlemore AS): Try the feeder or long pole for bream
Somerton (Oxford DAA): Regular match stretch, with roach, perch and skimmers
Angling Clubs/Tackle Shops & Permits: Littlemore AS (www.littlemoreanglingsociety.co.uk), Oxford & District AA (www.oxfordanglers.com), Try Olly's Tackle, Oxford (OX4 2QF) 07824 453489, Castaway Fishing Tackle, Banbury (OX16 2AB)

Royal Military Canal

Main Species: Roach, rudd, perch, tench, bream, carp, eels, pike
Notable Catches: Tench 6.5, Perch 2.0, Pike 24.06, Carp 32.00
Match record: 42.00lbs (mostly Bream)

An interesting and historic water, this canal was dug not for commerce but defence in the early 1800s, with the threat of invasion by Napoleon looming. There are even 'kinks' installed along its length intended as firing positions for defending troops! Despite huge criticism at the time, parts of it are now classed as an SSSI (with species such as emperor dragonflies and kingfishers), not to mention a beautiful spot for fishing in Kent. A good mix of species can be found, but it is especially well-regarded for its tench fishing. Do beware of changeable levels, especially in the winter when the depth drops away for flood prevention purposes.

Recommended Areas:
Seabrook to West Hythe (Cinque Ports AS): Well stocked, with many species, including some cracking carp, tench, pike.
West Hythe to Giggers Green (Cinque Ports AS): A wild, pretty section and a good bet for bream and tench in the deeps. Try pole and groundbait tactics.
Iden Lock to Appledore Dam (Rother FS): Plenty of tench, plus the odd large carp and pike.

Carp in excess of 30lb, like this one caught by Peter Gregory, are a genuine possibility on many canals, including the Royal Military.

Angling clubs/Tackle shops & Permits:
Cinque Ports AS (01303 891450) www.cinqueportsanglingsociety.org
Linton Angling Society (lintonangling.co.uk)
Rother Fishing Association (www.rfa.freeservers.com)
Tackle and Gun Shop, Tenterden, Kent (01580 764851)

Don't miss: For further visitors' info, corny jokes and fascinating facts, see www.royalmilitarycanal.com

Trivia

Never used for its intended defensive purpose, the Royal Military Canal was branded a huge white elephant at £234,410, a vast sum in Georgian England. Due to spiralling costs, it was only cut to half its planned width and depth in most places.

Wey Navigation Canal

Main species: Roach, bream, perch

Linking the Thames to the Basingstoke canal, this is a good stretch of under-fished water in the Weybridge and Byfleet area of Surrey. Much of the canal is run by a single club, which also holds the odd old school match on the Cut here. It has a fair flow to it, and often clear water making the central track a key area. For sheer numbers of bites, it probably can't rival the Basingstoke Canal, to which it connects, but savvy locals do track down some large perch and carp.

Recommended areas/Angling clubs/Shops: Weybridge AC (weybridgeac.webs.com), try Weybridge Guns and Tackle, KT13 9LB (01932 842675)

THE MIDLANDS

With a huge proliferation of man-made waterways, the Midlands could rightly be called the heartland of British canal fishing. The Birmingham area alone has more canals than Venice. The gondolas are missing, but there is a staggering amount of affordable and eye-opening fishing. So many canals exist that we couldn't hope to cover all, but for the adventurous angler there are miles of often free, totally underused fishing.

Handsome and deadlier than the Villa v West Brom derby: a Black Country zander.

Traditional canal matches are still going strong in some areas with winter matches regularly attracting 50-plus anglers, but equally, the specialist is well catered for. Large carp and chub are a feature on many waters, while the predator angler won't find a better range of canals to target zander, which are now well-established. Contrary to popular myth, this hasn't seen the end of silver fish sport. Skimmer populations in particular have exploded in recent times.

Ashby Canal
(aka Ashby-de-la-Zouch Canal)

Main species: Roach, perch, bream, tench, gudgeon, zander
Notable catches: Zander 18.00

A lockless 22 mile waterway connected to the Coventry Canal, this is a pretty rural water, but also one popular with boats. In part this is because it winds pleasantly through the landscape with no lock gates. Catches of small silvers can be good, and this and the coloured water also explain why there are plenty of zander.

Recommended areas:
Moira Furnace Museum & Country Park: Good for mixed nets; try pole with groundbait and pinkie, or bread in the winter.
Snarestone: Roach, skimmers and odd tench
Hinkley Area: Worth a try for zander – this is where the canal record fish came from!

Angling Clubs/Tackle Shops & Permits: Moira Furnace Museum and Country Park (DE12 6AT) sell tickets. Also fishing on the Waterway Wanderers Scheme

Birmingham Canal
(Birmingham Main Line Canal)

Main species: Roach, bream, perch, tench, pike, zander, carp

The Birmingham Canal is a fascinating urban waterway with several threads to it. Confusion can easily arise between sections. The New Main Line, for example, is a later development – a straight, state-of-the-art section developed to ease growing congestion. The 'old mainline' offers a curving alternative course. And in between, the canal has more arms than a military dictatorship, many of them small and totally under-fished. There is a huge amount of interesting, near-virgin water here for those who don't mind fishing in company. Virtually all the canal favourites feature, in addition to carp of well over 20lbs.

Recommended locations:
Old Mainline, Clissold Street: Skimmers and bonus tench.
New Main Line: Try around boats for perch, or pre-bait for carp.

Angling clubs/Tackle shops & Permits: Free fishing/Waterway Wanderers

Trivia

The Tardebigge lock flight on the Birmingham & Worcester Canal has 30 locks in two miles, the longest in the UK.

Birmingham & Fazeley Canal

Main species: Roach, bream, perch, pike, zander
Notable catches: Perch 2.08, Zander 14.00, Carp 35.00

The Fazeley and Tamworth area might be full of different waters, but few visitors seem to head to the canals. Like the other local Cuts, this is a cracking mixed fishery. The zander are one exciting option, but you'll also find swims here are packed with roach, perch and skimmers. As for the carp, these can run big: in 2012, match angler Dave Brown stormed to victory with a fish of 20lbs 14oz, landed on the pole!

Recommended locations:
Minworth, Birmingham (Birmingham AA): Skimmers and big perch feature here, try chopped worm.
Erdington (Birmingham AA): Groundbait and maggots work for decent bream.
The junction with the Coventry Canal, at Fazeley, is a good access point for various species, including the zander.

Angling clubs/Tackle shops & Permits: Birmingham AA (www.baa.co.uk), Tamworth Fishing Tackle, B79 7QE (01827 66701) are extremely helpful and well stocked in the area.

Birmingham & Worcester Canal

Main species: Roach, perch, bream, carp, zander
Notable catches: Carp 22.02, Perch 3.00

Running from the concrete of central Birmingham to green hills on the way to Worcester, this is a truly varied canal. Various methods work, with anglers taking some terrific carp on legered boilies, while pole fishermen catch some impressive nets of roach as well as big perch.

Recommended areas:
Astwood (Birmingham AA): good for both mixed fishing and the odd large carp.
Droitwich: Quality perch feature in mixed bags, with perch to just shy of 4lb. If it runs coloured, try chopped worm. Stoke Works is a popular match stretch: take casters for quality roach.
Perdiswell (Worcester DUAA): Productive for skimmers, roach and chub on pole.
Blackpole Bridge (Worcester DUAA): Good mixed fishing for roach, perch and gudgeon on fine tackle and bread punch or pinkie.
Stoke Works, Bromsgrove (Birmingham AA): Lots of small fish on the pole, but also holds some large carp.
Angling clubs/Tackle shops/Permits:
Worcester DUAA (www.wduaa.co.uk), Birmingham AA (www.baa.co.uk). Alan's Tackle, Worcester, WR2 4LG (01905 422107), Droitwich Angling WR9 8JB (01905 779300)

Caldon Canal

Main Species: Roach, perch, bream, carp

Part of the Trent and Mersey Canal, the Caldon can offer peaceful mixed fishing, with all the usual suspects plus the odd carp.

Recommended areas: Cromer Road and Lichfield Road (Goms Mill AS) are regular match locations. Pole fishing with fine tackle works best.
Angling clubs/Tackle shops/Permits:
Goms Mill AS: Tickets from Dolphin Discount Tackle, Stoke, ST4 4HW (01782 849390). Also stretches on the Waterway Wanderers Scheme.

Coventry Canal

Main Species: Roach, perch, bream, chub, zander, carp
Notable Catches: Carp 26.12, Zander 12.06, Chub 7.00

Another sometimes busy but fishy Midlands waterway with all manner of species. As well as classic species, zander are a viable target, as are chub. Rumours of a 9lb chub arrived in 2013, taken on a whole lobworm – and there are also carp here that seldom see a hook. Last but not least, there are good numbers of roach over 1lb on several stretches, usually taken on bread.

Recommended Areas:
Bedworth: A noted match stretch for chub.
Coventry Canal Basin: Urban, but worth a try for carp and bream, even in winter.

Trivia

The Coventry Canal was badly damaged by bombing in WW2, surviving only due to the great efforts of volunteers.

Chub are now a regular fixture in the Midlands. Try worm, caster or meat.

Fazely Junction to Sutton Road Bridge (Waterway Wanderers, Leamington AA): Worth a try for zander.
Hatton: Another noted zander area.
Angling clubs/Tackle shops/Permits: Leamington AA (www.leamington-angling.co.uk), Birmingham AA (www.baa.uk.com), Plough AS (www.ploughas.com), also some free water and Waterway Wanderers stretches. Enquire at local tackle shops, try WH Lane and Sons Coventry CV1 2JP (www.lanefishing.co.uk) (02476 223316) or at the Tamworth End, Tamworth Fishing Tackle B79 7QE (01827 66701)

Daw End Canal

Main species: Roach, perch, tench, bream, zander
Notable catches: Tench to 5lbs+

A branch of the Wyrley and Essington Canal, this is another hidden gem of the Midlands. Fishing for roach, skimmers and hybrids can be top drawer on light tackle, but do take heavier kit to target the resident bonus fish. Be prepared to walk and you'll find plenty of interesting areas, with the wides favourite for the water's secret but prolific stock of net fillers!

Recommended locations:
Try the Clayhanger Road Bridge section in Walsall WS8 7BN (Waterway Wanderers), where the wide sections produce fine nets of bream and tench.
Angling clubs/Tackle shops & Permits: Waterway Wanderers Scheme

Droitwich Canal

Main Species: Roach, perch, tench, bream, pike

Another interesting waterway, this is actually the amalgamation of two canals: the Droitwich Barge Canal and the Droitwich Junction Canal. The former is a broad canal, the latter much narrower. Restored in the 1970s, there are some classic canal swims here with typical lock gates

Recommended locations/Disabled access:
Porters Mill, Droitwich Spa (Droitwich Spa AA): Has secure platforms for disabled anglers and is a consistent spot for roach and skimmers. Try bread, pinkies and worm.

Angling clubs/Tackle shops & Permits: On the bank from Droitwich Spa AC, or try Droitwich Angling Centre WR9 8JB (01905 779300)

The 'Nine Locks' on the Dudley Number One, chub central.

Dudley No. 1 Canal *

Main species: Roach, perch, chub, pike, bream, gudgeon, carp
Notable catches: Chub 6.02, Carp 25.00

Of all the canals in the Midlands, the Dudley No.1 is perhaps the most deserving of its reputation as a big fish water. Don't let the busy nature and urban backdrop fool you; there are big chub here, with lots of fish over 3lb and the occasional monster twice that size.

The Dudley is also an historic area, a former area of great industry where old-timers still talk warmly about days when you could smell beer brewing from the towpath. Boat and human traffic can be an issue in holiday periods especially, but don't let that put you off. The fish will soon come back on the feed with the passing of boats and as well as specialist tactics, the stretch can also offer fun mixed fishing with roach, skimmers and even a few gudgeon.

Recommended locations: The Delph Locks, or 'Nine Locks' beside Brierley Hill are a particularly interesting section of canal. There are good-sized chub here,

along with the more usual suspects. Step up your tackle and try fishing worm, casters or a chunk of luncheon meat to any feature for the chub. Further up on Merry Hill Waterfront, large carp also feature for the dedicated specialist.
Angling clubs/Tackle shops & Permits: Look no further than Canal-side Tackle (DY5 2UA), which is a mine of both fishing supplies and friendly information on local fishing. www.fishology.co.uk (07779 012354)

Don't miss: *The Vine*, aka '*The Bull and Bladder*' (DY5 2TN) a fantastic old-school pub where it's still possible to get a perfect pint of local bitter and the biggest pork pie you've ever seen and still have plenty of change from a fiver.

Dudley No. 2 Canal

Main species: Roach, bream, perch, chub, carp, tench
Notable catches: Perch 4.00, Chub 5.08

Another cracking Midlands canal, this water produces mixed nets well into double figures for pole and waggler anglers, but is also becoming increasingly popular with specimen hunters. There are plenty of carp here, including fish over 20lb.

Recommended locations: Off Chancel Way, Halesowen: A good range of species. Try worm for big perch, or boilies for chub and carp.

Angling Clubs/Tackle Shops & Permits: £2 on the bank. Mal Storey Angling Centre, Halesowen (B63 4QQ) 0121 5501830

Erewash Canal

Main species: Roach, bream, perch, tench, chub, carp

Cutting through both suburban and leafier stretches, the Erewash Canal is a dependable water for bites year-round. Pollution has been a problem with a serious fire in recent history, but stocks are bouncing back.

Recommended locations:
Gallows Bridge, Ilkestone/Pasture Lock (Notts AA): Good areas to try for 'bits' but also skimmers and bonus chub.
Angling clubs/Tackle shops & Permits: Scunthorpe AA, Permits from Scunthorpe Angling Centre (01724 849815)
Nottingham AA (www.nottinghamanglers.co.uk)

Gloucester Canal *

Main species: Roach, bream, carp, pike, zander
Notable catches: Grass carp 31.08, Pike 38.00 (rumoured), Zander 14.03
Match record: 47.00 bream

Another beast of a canal, the Gloucester is a broad and deep channel that perhaps suits the determined, proactive angler best. Particularly noted for its predator fishing, it is popular with lure and deadbait anglers – not surprising as it is the closest

The Gloucester Canal is a good bet for bigger canal fish of all species, not least of all predators.

venue to the south west with any substantial population of zander.

There is vast, untapped water here, and uncaught monsters. The carp and pike are two particular key species which have plenty of space to hide and relatively few rods chasing them. Bream are also out in force and, with heavy ground baiting, nets of 200lbs have been caught on the Gloucester.

Recommended areas:
Hempstead (Winget AC): Noted match area, produces mixed bags. Try pole or feeder and pellet or maggot.
Sharpness end, Purton: Terrific in spring for big bream catches.
Cambridge Arms: pike carp, bream.
Frampton Area: Three miles here include

Bream stocks are back to their best on various stretches the Grand Union.

the main boating junction, and several other areas excellent for late season roach and bream, not to mention pike.

Angling clubs/Tackle shops/Permits: Winget AC, GUAA (Gloucester United Angling Associations), also stretches on the Waterway Wanderers permit.
For further info and tickets try the friendly staff at Lobby's Tackle, Stonehouse GL10 2NA (01453 791417)

Grand Union Canal *

Main species: Roach, bream, tench, perch, gudgeon, carp
Notable catches: Chub 6.00, Carp 46.04, Zander 12.00

In terms of sheer size and variety, the Grand Union could easily be called the daddy of all Britain's canals, with 166 locks and more pegs than you could fish in a lifetime. Serving as a main artery between Birmingham and London, it was a hugely important waterway in Britain's industrial development.

The Grand Union itself is a great connecting channel, consisting of a number of different canals. Where names differ, specific information on different branches can be found under separate headings, for example the Regent's Canal in London, at the southern end.

Today, you'll find a vast amount of fishing and a mind-boggling number of angling clubs and fish species, with stretches running through cute, leafy villages as well as distinctly urban places. It is still prolific for catching classic nets of roach and bream if you know where to look. The days of heavy industry might be long gone, but much of the canal is still well-used by boats, so water clarity can be an issue and the successful angler must be adaptable here. Bread punch works in the winter, but for coloured water, continental groundbait and baits such as worm, pinkie and maggot are essential.

Recommended areas:
Catherine-De-Barnes, Solihull: between bridges 77-78 excellent for roach and skimmers. Bread punch works well, or pinkie if the water is heavily coloured. Also some carp and tench. (100 AC)
Knowle Locks (100 AC): Good for roach, squat or pinkie over groundbait.
Blisworth Village, Northants (Northampton Nene AC): Good for mixed nets, plus big perch on chopped worm.
Countesthorpe Road Bridge, Wigston (Wigston AS): Lots of tree cover and tench here. Fish bigger baits such as corn or caster on heavier tackle.
Leamington Spa (LACC): Twelve miles of excellent lure fishing for predators, plus good silver fish stocks and carp to over 20lbs.
Market Harborough, Leicester (Wreake AC): Good mixed bags of roach, perch, gudgeon and bonus bream around Great Bowden.

Trivia

At 137 miles, the Grand Union Canal is Britain's longest. Together with connected waterways, the route would hit a colossal 286 miles.

Lure fanatic Andy Mytton cradles a typical canal zander. The 'Lure Anglers Canal Club' (LACC) have some of the best water on the Grand Union.

Gudgeon provide old school fun on the Grand Union.

Angling clubs/Tackle shops & Permits:
Lure Anglers Canal Club (www.lureanglerscanalclub.co.uk) Buy tickets online.
100 AC – Tickets from K.J. Angling (01217 476962)
Northampton Nene AC (01604 761173)
Wigston AS (07860 112000)
Wreake AC – Tickets from Oadby Angling (LE2 5DN)
Also see the Waterway Wanderers Scheme.

Don't miss: For a taste of nostalgia, Stoke Bruerne (South of Northampton) is a living remnant of Britain's watery past with canalside pubs and cafes, historic places and the Canal Museum (www.stokebruernecanalmuseum.org.uk).

See www.canalrivertrust.org.uk for more info.

Grantham Canal

Main species: Roach, bream, perch, carp, tench, pike

Another unsung Midlands canal that offers some productive swims and the chance of a decent mixed bag. In places it can get very shallow and weedy, but the fish are there. Tench, as well as roach and bream will turn up if you use simple old-school tactics and baits such as bread and corn. As a non-navigable canal you are also guaranteed a day free of barges!

Recommended locations:
Bottesford, Grantham (Bottesford AA): Look for gaps in the weed for fine tench.
Cotgrave Road Section (Notts AA): A productive area for roach and tench, especially in early mornings.
Smite Aqueduct to Hose (Notts AA): The canal is shallow, weedy and while this might not be armchair fishing, it is a quiet area with plenty of bites to be had. Try pole or waggler and maggots.
Angling clubs/Tackle shops/Permits:
Nottingham AA (www.nottinghamanglers.co.uk), Bottesford AA, Grantham AA, - Tickets from Grantham Angling Centre NG31 6JQ (01476 575622)

Llangollen Canal

Main species: Roach, dace, perch, gudgeon, bream, carp
Notable catches: Perch 2.02,

As this rather picturesque waterway passes into the Midlands, the range of species gets even more interesting. Perhaps the most alluring and of unknown quantity are the carp, with fish rumoured into the low 30s, if you can find them!

Recommended areas:
Wrenbury (Lymm AC): Can throw up a whole range of species with pike and carp as well as plenty of roach and bream.

Angling clubs/Tackle shops & Permits: Lymm AC (www.lymmanglersclub.com)

Newport Canal, Shropshire

*

Main species: Roach, rudd, perch, crucians, carp

The Newport offers an excellent chance of a canal crucian, as Alan Smallman shows.

Pretty as a picture and stuffed with a wide range of species, the Newport Canal is a delightful place to fish. One advantage is a lack of boat access, making for peaceful fishing. Several clubs each run separate, enclosed stretches where interesting stocking policies have led to great mixed fishing, as well as fairly regular matches.

The highlight of my own visit here was meeting veteran angler Alan Smallman, who still cycles the towpath with his tackle in his 80s, having caught his very first fish, a perch, here *before* World War II! Today, there are several curious additions to target aside from traditional species; this is the place to catch a canal crucian! It can fish hard on a bright day, so try early and late in the spring and summer months.

A real 'lucky dip', the Shropshire Newport has a wealth of species.

Recommended locations:
Vineyard Road (Audco AC): A lovely stretch with lilies and a wide range of species, including rudd, tench and crucians. Pole or light waggler tactics work a treat.
Angling clubs/Tackle shops & Permits: Audco AC (www.audcoac.co.uk),
Telford Angling Association, tickets from Newport Tackle TF10 7AU (01952 820334), also see www.telfordwebs.co.uk/fishing for other clubs and ticket/tackle outlets.

Nottingham & Beeston Canal (aka 'Beeston Canal')

Main Species: Roach, bream, chub, perch, pike, carp

Joined at each end by the River Trent, this is an interesting little canal with river visitors joining the usual canal coarse fish. Large chub, as well as occasional carp have been known to show up in catches. Access is decent too, with well cut towpaths. It has a good flow on it, owing partly to the fact that water is drawn from here to be superheated and used to keep Nottingham warm and powered. The steady tow lends itself to pole or even stick float fishing.

Recommended locations:
Beeston, Notts (Notts AA): Bream as well as decent numbers of small barbel feature here. Try worm on the Boots outfall area.

Angling clubs/Tackle shops & Permits: Nottingham AA (www.nottinghamanglers.co.uk), Try Gerry's of Nottingham NG7 3BN (0115 9781695)

Skimmer populations are thriving across the Midlands at present.

Oxford Canal
(see also London and South)

Main species: Roach, bream, gudgeon, zander, perch, chub, carp
Notable catches: Zander 12.08

The top end of the Oxford Canal is as prolific as the south in places. Zander are a particular attraction; and populations of roach and other canal favourites are now also back in a healthy balance.

Recommended areas:
Rugby Town Centre: Worth roving for both carp and zander to double figures.
Hillmorton: Silver fish shoals here, also some predators.
Hawkesbury Junction/Longford, Coventry (Waterway Wanderers): Worth roving for zander – try boats and structures.
Angling clubs/Tackle shops:
Waterway Wanderers scheme, also some free fishing. Try Rugby Tackle CV22 7DS (01788 544913) or WH Lane & Son, Coventry CV1 2JP (02476 223316)

Shropshire Union Canal *

Main species: Roach, perch, bream, tench, chub, carp
Notable catches: Perch 4.0, Bream 5.14, Chub 5.00
Match record: 107.00lbs (Carp) Paul Turner, Autherley

The Shropshire Union Canal is, rather confusingly, the name given to an amalgamation of various canal branches spanning from the Midlands right into Wales. To avoid an almighty muddle, we refer to branches such as the Montgomery and Chester Canals under their separate, better-known names.

The 'Shroppie' itself is a venue of wide renown, having staged the National Angling Championships on more than one occasion. All the usual canal species can be found, but a really notable presence are the chub. Released in great numbers to boost catches, these fish have grown on to reach impressive sizes. Odd carp also feature and run large. But it is not all about big fish and this is also a canal where gudgeon can and do sometimes turn up in vast numbers.

Boat traffic is one aspect that can deter anglers from this venue, hence an early start can be a good idea. Nevertheless, locals are not put off and another notable aspect of the canal is the thriving competition scene, with regular winter matches at weekends.

As well as quantity, the Shroppie has quality including some belting chub, carp and perch.

Trivia

The Shropshire Union is said to be Britain's 'Most Haunted Fishery'. Numerous towpath sightings include a fighter pilot, Roman Centurion and a drowned boatman. Pack a crucifix in your seatbox.

Recommended areas:
Norbury Junction, Staffs (Stoke City AA) is probably the best-known stretch for match and pleasure anglers. Bites galore here with roach, gudgeon and skimmers on small baits, as well as bonus chub to features.
Church Eaton (Stafford AA): Noted area for bream and skimmers.
Pendeford (Wolverhampton AA): A good head of carp join the other species here, regarded as one of the best canal match stretches in the entire Midlands.

Angling clubs/Tackle shops & Permits: Stoke City AA (Contact chairman: 01782 818380) Lymm AC (www.lymmanglersclub.com), Stafford AA, Wolverhampton AA (www.wolverhamptonaa.co.uk)

Don't miss: *The Junction Inn* ST20 0PN (01785 284288) is slap bang by the canal, offers a decent pint and is also the meeting point for weekend match anglers. There is further fishing info on their site: www.norburyjunction.com

Soho Loop Canal

Main species: Roach, bream, perch, carp

Another reliable Cut in the Birmingham area, boasting free fishing for tidy nets of roach, as well as bonus skimmers and bream. This water fishes especially well in the summer on typical canal tactics, such as pole fished pinkie and caster.

Recommended areas:
Winson Green (Free Fishing) for roach and bream. Try swims with overhanging trees. Don't forget groundbait and casters for the better fish.

Angling clubs/Tackle shops & Permits: Black Country AS, also some free fishing with EA Licence

Staffordshire & Worcester Canal

Main species: Roach, bream, perch, ruffe, gudgeon, chub, carp
Notable catches: Perch 3.04, Chub 6.15, Carp 29.00
Match record: 92.00lbs (chub), Eric Gardner, Planks Lane, Wombourne 2010

Another of Britain's great untapped fisheries, this classic narrowboat canal runs for some 46 miles, linking the River Severn at Stourport with the Trent and Mersey Canal at Great Haywood. There is a good variety of sport, from regular matches held by several clubs, through to some challenging but rewarding specimen fishing. There are some cracking chub in places, as well as surprises like carp and zander.

Trivia

The Staffordshire Championships are quite possibly England's oldest fishing match, having been staged on the 'Shroppie' Canal since the 1800s.

Recommended areas: *Boat Inn* and *Cross Keys* pub, Penkridge: for perch and chub.
Awbridge Bridge, Wombourne (Wolverhampton AA): A noted area for chub.
Acton Trussell, Staffs (Wolverhampton DAA): Chopped worm and caster take decent chub and perch to over 2lb here.
Oldington Lane, Kidderminster (Birmingham AA): Mixed bags of roach, perch and gudgeon on small baits. Ideal stretch to take the kids with a whip.
Gailey, Staffs (Wolverhampton AA): Bite-a-chuck fishing for small species on pinkies or squats.
Oxley Marina (Wolverhampton DAA): Quality year-round roach and bream fishing. Try bread or caster for the better samples.
Stafford (Izaak Walton AA): All the usual species, plus some huge carp.
Tixall Wides (Potteries AS):

Angling clubs/Tackle shops & Permits: Wolverhampton AA (Day tickets on the bank)/Archline Angling Ltd (01543 426158) Birmingham AA (www.baa.uk.com) Permits from Mark's Tackle, Stourport on Severn, (DY13 8UU) or Ian's Tackle (01785 715744)

Stratford-upon-Avon Canal

Main species: Roach, perch, bream, pike
Noted catches: Tench 5.12

Another classic restored narrowboat canal, the Stratford fishes well for a range of species. Anglers tend to favour autumn, when boat traffic slows down. There are 26 miles of water divided into two main sections. There are various locks, bridges and other typical features, as well as the rather novel 'Shirley Drawbridge' (Bridge no.8), which flips upwards to let boats pass.

Recommended areas: Lapworth: Produces roach, bream and even the odd crucian.
Bishopton Lane: Tench can sometimes be found in this section, along with roach shoals.

Angling clubs/Tackle shops & Permits: Free Fishing/Waterway Wanderers

Stroudwater Canal

Main species: Roach, perch, tench, pike

Restoration is on-going on this pretty canal, which is much shallower and clearer than the nearby Gloucester Canal. In the past it has produced some excellent tench and pike fishing in particular.

Recommended locations:
Thrupp/Ryeford: Good mixed fishing, including tench and pike.

Angling clubs/Tackle shops & Permits: Stroud DAA, tickets from Lobby's Tackle, Stonehouse GL10 2NA (01453 791417)

Stourbridge Canal

Main species: Roach, perch, bream, pike, chub
Notable catches: Roach 2.00, Perch 3.01, Carp 30.00

Once used for transporting glassware via Stourbridge to the rest of the Midlands canal network, this represents a fishy and under-fished stretch of water that still sees some matches and good nets of fish.

Recommended locations:
Canal Street, Stourbridge: Top fishing just a short cast from Stourbridge town centre. Try whip and small baits for plenty of bites, or worm and caster on the far bank for larger residents

Angling clubs/Tackle shops & Permits: Halesowen Royal British Legion, tickets available on the bank.

Tame Valley Canal

Main species: Roach, perch, bream, carp, pike
Notable catches: Perch 2.08, Pike 15.04

A late addition to the Birmingham network of canals in 1844, this Cut offers some cheap and seriously under-fished water. Stocks are an unknown quantity in many areas, but as well as roach, some large perch and carp have been spotted.

Recommended areas: Tame Valley to Salford Junction at Gravelly Hill: Try fishing a whip or pole for mixed bags, or soft rubber lures for predators.
Angling clubs/Tackle shops & Permits: Waterway Wanderers

Trent & Mersey Canal
(also see North section)

Main species: Roach, perch, gudgeon, bream, zander, carp
Notable catches: Roach 2.01, Zander 10.00, Carp 27.08

One of England's longest canals, the Trent and Mersey holds an interesting mix of species and areas. The Midlands end of this 93½ mile long waterway starts at the River Trent: little surprise then, that bonus chub and the odd large pike are found at this end. Zander are also now established, with fish to low double figures a realistic target. It can be a busy place, with both boat users and also as part of the National Cycle Network around towns such as Stoke on Trent. Don't let this put you off however: there is some truly excellent mixed fishing at a knock-down price. At the time of printing, Burton Mutual Angling Association offer one of the best value season tickets in England at just £12 (or £1 for U18s!)

Recommended areas:
Dallow Lock (Burton Mutual AA): Has skimmers, chub and large roach. Try caster and worm; or deadbaits for zander.
Armitage, Staffs (Coors AC): Lots of small fish to pinkies, plus odd large perch.
Hoo Mill to Great Haywood (Izaak Walton AA): Mixed catches year round.
Whieldon Rd (Stoke) to Meaford Bottom Lock (Fenton DAA) : Most species present here and a productive year round fishery, with winter nets to 40lbs!

Angling clubs/Tackle shops & Permits:
Burton Mutual Angling Association (07891 126910), Fenton DAA (www.fentonanddistrictanglingsociety.co.uk), Coors AC – Tickets from Burton Angling Supplies DE14 2DA (www.burtonangling.co.uk)
Izaak Walton AA (www.iwsaa.co.uk)

Walsall Canal

Main Species: Roach, perch, bream, tench

Yet another unsung Midlands Cut, where sheltered urban spots produce decent bread and butter fishing even in winter frosts. Records are scant, apart from the occasional match, but light pole tackle is a safe bet for mixed catches year round.

Recommended areas: Birchills, Walsall (Waterway Wanderers): try pinkies, punched bread or bloodworm for winter roach.
Ocker Hill, Tipton, West Mids (Waterway Wanderers): Good winter punch fishing for roach, plus resident pike.
Angling clubs/Tackle shops/Permits: Waterway Wanderers/Free fishing

Wednesbury Old Canal

Main Species: Roach, perch, bream, pike

Parts of this waterway became derelict in the 1960s, but some highly-fishable water still exists, such as around Pudding Green Junction. Expect the usual canal species, and enjoy some seriously under-exploited fishing!

Recommended locations: Ryders Green area for mixed catches on fine float tackle.
Angling clubs/Tackle shops & Permits: Waterway Wanderers

Wyrley & Essington Canal

Main species: Roach, perch, tench, pike, carp

Some peaceful fishing here on the waterway known by locals as the 'Curly Wyrley' canal. With little boat traffic for much of the season, the water is often clear and the atmosphere relaxing. Pike and occasional large carp feature, in addition to the classic roach, skimmers and perch. The real highlight however is the tench fishing, and there are some cracking fish here if you're prepared to go and find them. Bread and casters are always worth having.

Recommended locations:
Pelsall (Cashmores AC): Cracking mixed fishing. Roach, tench and perch reach good sizes here.
Angling clubs/Tackle shops & Permits: Cashmores AC (Club Secretary: 01922 413925) or www.simplematchfishing.co.uk. Also try the Waterway Wanderers Scheme, which includes several stretches of low cost fishing.

WALES

The canals of Wales are a well-kept secret when it comes to fishing. Visitors know about great rivers such as the Wye and Usk, and yet drive straight past some of the most picturesque, not to mention under-fished, canals you'll find anywhere in Britain. Restoration efforts have paid dividends and it could be said that the Welsh canals have undergone something of a renaissance at the start of the 21st Century. Like the West Country, clear, rural waters are a special highlight and waterways such as the Monmouth and Brecon, as well as the Montgomery and Llangollen canals offer some classic fishing for traditional species such as roach and bream in particular, not to mention wonderful views and rich history.

Llangollen Canal

Main species: Roach, rudd, perch, bream, tench, pike, chub, carp
Notable catches: Roach 2.01

From its namesake town in Wales, this is a canal with a pedigree for big roach in particular. Outside peak summer season and weekends are the most peaceful times for fishing. The better fish can be wily and with regular tow often on the water, this can feel like a small river, so a careful presentation is a must. In clearer conditions, try bread. It's not all roach though: there are some fair perch and chub if you can find them, along with most other canal species.

Recommended areas: Llangollen town and surrounding area is always worth a cast. Travel light and carry polarising glasses to spot the fish.
The Dusty Miller pub, Wrenbury cum Frith: Great place for winter roach and dace. Try to cover obstacles such as boats for quality perch.
Angling clubs/Tackle shops & Permits: Llangollen Angling Association, Permits can be purchased from the newsagents/fishing tackle shop at 12 Chapel St, Llangollen (01978 860155). The Waterway Wanders scheme also has several stretches.

Don't miss: The Pontcysyllte Aqueduct *(below)* is an incredible feat of engineering, not to mention an absolute must-see for the canal enthusiast. See www.pontcysyllte-aqueduct.co.uk for more fascinating details on this World Heritage Site.

Monmouthshire & Brecon Canal *

Main species: Roach, perch, bream, tench, rudd
Notable catches: Chub 7.03, Roach 1.15

One of the most beautiful canals in Britain, this waterway is also one of the most lightly fished considering the huge number of swims. For much of its length it is dainty, running through a backdrop of steep-sided valleys and pretty villages. Due to the uneven terrain, its course is long and full of picturesque curves. The range of species is huge and mysterious; everything from dace to koi carp have shown up in the various stretches. Bread and butter fishing for roach can be excellent down the track, while wider sections and classic bends tend to produce bream. Pike have been elusive in past decades, but are now on the increase with the odd large fish as well as jacks increasingly present in the rural stretches.

Recommended areas:
Goytre: is a good bet for roach fishing. Try bread punch in winter.
Ty Coch: has a real variety of swims, with locks and pounds. It has produced carp and chub as well as the usual suspects in the past.
High Cross (en route to Newport): has some nice weedy swims and resident tench.

Angling clubs/Tackle shops & Permits: A mixture of Waterway Wanderers stretches and free fishing.
Cwmbran Angling, Gwent, NP44 1EQ (01633 868890)

Trivia

The 'Mon and Brec' as locals call it, is actually the modern name for two 18th century canals, The Monmouthshire and The Brecknock & Abergavenny.

Don't miss: The Fourteen Locks Canal Centre, near Newport (www.fourteen-locks.co.uk) offers a welcome stop-off point with art displays and a café, as well as a place to delve into the history of the canal.

Young angler Mackenzie Morris admires a canal roach from the 'Mon and Brec'.

The Montgomery Canal *

Main species: Roach, rudd, bream, tench, pike

Notable catches: Chub 5.00, Roach 1.10

Another absolute gem of a canal, the 'Monty' as locals affectionately call it is a place of meandering beauty. Connected to the Shropshire Union, it is also a tale of successful restoration. There are both urban sections, with boats running, as well as painfully shallow, and painfully beautiful, rural sections running through stunning Welsh countryside. The urban sections, especially through Welshpool, are fine spots for bigger fish. Stocks can be patchier out of the towns, but there are good roach, plenty of jack pike and even the odd chub lurking.

Recommended areas: Slap bang in the centre of Welshpool is prolific for roach as well as bonus bream and tench. Try the wider areas with bread on the hook. Out of town, the water gets clearer but fish can be patchier, so be prepared to rove. Access is not always simple, but try the *Three Horseshoes* pub or side roads on the way to Garthmyl. These stretches are perfect for simple sight fishing, and ideal flyfishing territory for roach and pike.

Disabled access: Try Welshpool town centre, where there are level banks and street access.

Angling clubs/Tackle shops & Permits: The Montgomery Angling Association run the fishing, but the Tourist Information Centre SY21 7DD at Welshpool sells day permits (01938 552043)

Don't miss: The Powysland Museum and Canal Centre (Welshpool), is right on the banks of the Monty and well worth a stop off.

There are some real net-fillers to be caught right in Welshpool town. Try a pinch of bread flake.

The idyllic Montgomery Canal stretches through some beautiful countryside. The fish can be spread out in the rural sections, so do travel light.

NORTH OF ENGLAND

Northern England is an area rich in canal history. In fact, northerners could lay a reasonable claim to both Britain's earliest and latest canals in the Bridgewater and Manchester Ship Canals respectively. There are also unsung waters galore, and a tremendous variety, with both pretty countryside canals yet also some surprisingly prolific urban hot spots. Don't expect purely traditional 'bread and butter' fishing either: large carp and even game fish are there to be found for the adventurous. In terms of canal fishing it really isn't so grim up North.

As well as the clubs and links below, www.yorkshirefishing.net has an excellent section on canals.

Aire & Calder Navigation Canal

Main species: Roach, perch, bream, chub, pike, gudgeon, tench, carp
Notable catches: Chub 5.00, Carp 25.00
Match record: 97.11lbs (bream and chub)

This great Yorkshire canal is one of the most interesting mixed fisheries in the north of England with a terrific variety of swims and species. It is still known for its classic roach fishing, with nets to 30lbs plus a possibility on hemp or caster, but you might catch anything from dace to big carp. Strictly speaking of course, it's a navigation channel and a mighty one at that, with depths typically 12ft down the central track. For this reason, long pole and feeder tactics tend to be the staple methods.

Another refreshing feature of the Aire and Calder is a healthy match fishing scene and proactive local anglers. At the time of writing some 100 fishing platforms have been installed between Heck and New Bridge (that's one 'heck' of a lot!). As a major 'ship canal', the venue also still sees regular usage from huge barges transporting raw materials, making early, late or weekend sessions a good plan.

Recommended locations:
Great Heck/Pollington (Boothferry Aire and Calder Joint Canal Committee): Pollington is a superb area for roach, particularly pegs 405 to 420, with a positive groundbait and hemp, caster or maggot approach yielding some cracking catches. Great Heck also has roach, but with the added bonus of some big resident chub.
Woodleford, Leeds Centre (Leeds & District ASA): Plenty of pegs here, with good depths right down to 15ft in places and boat moorings. Feeder tactics score well and you could catch anything from tench and carp to the odd stray barbel!
Altofts (Mirfield AC): Try maggot and caster for roach.

Disabled access: Great Heck has parking and wheelchair-friendly pegs.

Angling clubs/Tackle shops & Permits: Boothferry Aire and Calder Joint Canal Committee (bacjcccanalfishing.co.uk),

Mirfield AC (mirfieldac.co.uk), permits from Chris Roberts Tackle, Huddersfield (01484 545032), Leeds and District ASA (www.leedsdasa.co.uk)

Ashton Canal

Main species: Roach, perch, ruffe, bream, carp, tench

Connected to the Huddersfield Narrow Canal, there are over six miles of water here and many lock gates holding most traditional canal species. The Ashton area itself has a reputation for being a bit 'tasty' with plenty of trolleys and urban sights. Early morning sessions still produce fish and avoid trouble.

Recommended areas:
Lumb Lane: Produces decent roach and bream nets
Portland Basin: Roach, pike and odd carp.

Angling clubs/Tackle shops & Permits: Try the Waterway Wanderers Scheme,
More tickets and local info at Spec-Tackle in Ashton-under-Lyme (OL6 6BZ)

Bardsley Canal
(aka 'Hollinwood Canal')

Main species: Roach, perch, bream, carp

Notable catches: Carp 25.00

A mere 300 yards of pretty canal survive at Daisy Nook Park, which also once connected to the so-called Hollinwood Canal. Restoration remains a possibility in this pretty area but for the present, Limehurst Angling Club run an attractive and well-stocked little stretch of water.

Recommended areas: Daisy Nook Park, Oldham: Simple float fishing tactics with maggots bring plenty of bites from a range of species here.

Angling clubs/Tackle shops & Permits: Limehurst AC (Day tickets available on the bank)

Don't miss: The park itself is a tranquil place for a walk or just a quiet loaf.

Barnsley Canal

Main species: Carp, roach, perch, bream

Despite whole sections of this cute canal falling into disrepair, some fine restoration work has seen stretches return as a well stocked coarse fishery.

Recommended areas: Try around Stockport itself for roach, pinkies or bread punch.

Angling clubs/Tackle shops & Permits: Stockport and District AA, tickets and info from Hazel Grove Angling Centre, Stockport SK7 6DG (01625 858643)

Beverley Canal

Main Species: Carp, roach, perch, bream, tench

Not a long Cut, but a good one, offering a slice of traditional canal fishing here, with specimen perch and even the odd ide as well as good roach fishing.

Recommended areas: Beverley (Hull DAA): Pole fishing with small baits for the roach, or you should try a worm for perch to 2lb plus.

Angling clubs/Tackle shops & Permits: Hull DAA (www.hdaafishing.co.uk)

Brampton Canal

Main species: Roach, perch, bream, crucians, tench, carp

Notable catches: Roach 1.08, Perch 3.02, Tench 5.04

Another cute, disused waterway restored for fishing, there are good mixed stocks here, with everything from fair-sized roach and perch to double figure carp.

Recommended areas: Access near Brampton Road, plenty of pegs for consistent mixed fishing.

Angling clubs/Tackle shops & Permits: Barnsley DAA (barnsley-fishing.co.uk), try Barnsley Bait Co S75 6YS (01226 210183) for tickets.

Bridgewater Canal

Main species: Roach, bream, perch, pike, odd large carp

Notable catches: Carp 30.00, Roach 2.00

The Bridgewater Canal was pivotal in the growth of Manchester, opened by coal tycoon Francis Egerton to shift the black stuff from Worsley to Manchester (over 60,000 tons were sent down the canal in 1761 alone). These days heavy industry is absent but the Cut remains a pretty and historic remnant of Industrial Revolution England, also connecting to several other waterways in the 'Cheshire Ring' including the Rochdale and Manchester Ship Canals. It has good variety, with some fine carp hiding along with the usual canal staples.

Recommended locations:

Higher Green, Astley (Warrington AA): Roach and tench here. Try hemp and worm respectively.

Kraft Arm at Watersmeet (Hulme Hall Road, Manchester) for good bream fishing and occasional carp.

Preston Brook Marina, Warrington (Lymm AC): Big roach, pike and carp.

Angling clubs/Tackle shops & Permits: Lymm AC (lymmanglersclub.co.uk), Warrington AA (www.warrington-anglers.org.uk). £20 a year Manchester Ship Canal permit, try Trafford Angling Supplies (01618 641211)

.........Trivia.........

The Bridgewater is arguably Britain's earliest 'true' canal, opened in 1761.

Calder & Hebble Canal

(aka Calder and Hebble Navigation)

Main species: Roach, perch, bream, pike, eels

Match record: 24.11 (Bream and skimmers)

This broad waterway in West Yorkshire very nearly didn't happen at all. A tale of local and Parliamentary objections and borrowed money, its history is a triumph of northern grit and stubbornness! Just as well, because today it offers some cracking match-style fishing as well as decent winter pike and perch.

Recommended areas: Bingley Arms Bridge (Wakefield AC): Roach and tench feature here, with casters a favourite local bait.
Horbury Bridge (Wakefield AC): Chub feature here, as well as the usual suspects.
Dewsbury (Dewsbury AC): Mixed fishing, also decent for pike and perch to lures.

Angling clubs/Tackle shops & Permits: Wakefield AC (www.wakefieldac.co.uk), Tickets from Bob Co Tackle (01924 279880), Dewsbury AC (dewsburyanglingclub.co.uk), Tickets from Graham's Tackle, Batley WF17 8PN (01924 442040)

Chester Canal

see Shropshire Union Canal

Chesterfield Canal

Main species: Roach, perch, bream, chub

Another canal where fishing pressure, or reliable catch records, are scant, the Chesterfield is said to hold the odd carp these days, as well as the usual species.

Recommended areas:
Clayworth Boat Yard (Worksop DAA): Big bream and chub. Catapults are banned, so pole fishing works best with cupped feed.

Permits: Worksop DAA (Tickets on the bank). Also see Waterway Wanderers scheme.

An unusual canal fish, but grayling are common in the clear waters of the Driffield.

Driffield Canal

Main Species: Roach, perch, trout, grayling, carp, pike
Notable Catches: Grayling 3.14, Rainbow Trout 6.08

This secluded venue boasts clear water and some of the most remarkable fish stocks of any canal in the UK! Flyfishing is as valid as float fishing for stocks of trout and grayling, which run to good sizes here. Take a pair of polarising glasses and you'll also spot decent roach, pike and odd carp.

Recommended locations: Wansford Village (Hull DAA): As good a starting point as any. Try roving with a fly rod or float tackle.

Angling clubs/Tackle shops & Permits: Hull DAA (www.hdaafishing.co.uk)

Ellesmere Canal

See Shropshire Union Canal

Fossdyke Canal

Main Species: Roach, perch, bream
Notable Catches: Perch 4.11 (unconfirmed), Carp 26.00

First built by the Romans in around 120 AD, this is a truly ancient man-made waterway – although experts disagree on whether it can be classed as a true canal, to say nothing of its ambiguous origins and reworking over many centuries. Running for 12 miles to connect the rivers Witham and Trent, the fishing can be almost as interesting as the history, with excellent pleasure fishing but also a healthy match scene. Along with a good head of roach and skimmers, some huge perch have been landed including a reputed fish of 4.11lbs! A 2lb fish is always possible, so don't leave home without a tub of worms.

Recommended locations: Woodcocks (Lincoln DAA) for mixed catches, pole and maggots effective for skimmers, perch and roach.
Torksey (Lincoln DAA) is a good winter holding area for silver fish on pinkies. Matches here are often won with double figure bags on the pole.

Angling Clubs/Tackle Shops & Permits: Lincoln DAA (ldaa.webs.com), tickets from Harrisons Tackle (01522 523834)

Huddersfield Broad Canal
*

Main Species: Roach, perch, bream, pike, chub, tench
Notable Catches: Chub 3lbs, Roach 1.10

By 'eck – a bonus fish stretches the elastic on the Huddersfield Broad Canal.

Don't be put off by bricks and the odd bit of litter: the canals of the North are undergoing a real renaissance.

Running through central Huddersfield, this is one of the most urban waterways you could lay eyes on. But don't be fooled and don't follow my grandfather's advice ('Lord deliver me from Hell, Hull and Huddersfield') because there is some belting fishing to be had. There is still a healthy match fishing scene here, where the likes of England international Denis White have graced contests, taking classic canal bags of roach as well as bonus fish such as bream and chub. Another welcome feature are the pike. Don't expect miracles, but there are many jacks in the 1-4lb bracket as well as the odd bigger fish. A light lure outfit gives maximum sport but cheap, single hook lures save heartache with discarded junk.

Recommended locations: Try right through the town centre for mixed nets. Around the gasworks for roach and perch, pole fished caster and pinkie. Roving with lures or small deadbaits best for pike.

Angling clubs/Tackle shops & Permits: Mirfield AC (www.mirfieldac.co.uk)

Huddersfield Narrow Canal

Main species: Roach, bream, perch, chub, carp

Match record: 64.00 (chub)

Many locks and some twenty miles of lightly-fished water make up this canal. There is some prime roach fishing, but also good numbers of carp in some of the shorter sections, which respond to pellets and meat as well as traditional baits. Chub also feature if you know where to find them.

Recommended locations: Try between the locks in Slaithewaite, for nets of chub and bream.
Greenfield Lock (Saddleworth AA): Roach, skimmers and perch here.
Diggle: Noted match stretch, with chub among excellent mixed nets

Angling clubs/Tackle shops & Permits: Slaithewaite DAA, tickets from Chris Roberts Tackle, Slaithewaite (01484 545032), Saddleworth AA, tickets from Sheddings Angling Supplies (01613 452761)

Lancaster Canal
(aka Kendal Lancaster Canal)

Main species: Roach, perch, tench, bream, pike, grass carp

Notable catches: Tench 7.00, Grass Carp 22.00

A scenic and often secluded northern waterway, this distinguished old Cut runs through some lovely countryside. Non-navigable at the Tewitfield section, much of its waters are clear, weedy and peaceful. Tench and pike both thrive here, but perhaps the most interesting species are grass carp, that can be challenging but run to an excellent size.

Recommended locations:
Holme & Burton (Waterway Wanderers): Just off the A6070 you'll find superbly wild fishing. Roving works best. Try deadbaits or flies for pike; bread or boilies for the tench and grass carp.
Stainton to Tewitfield (KDAC): Good nets of roach and perch, as well as a great chance for a grass carp.
Pike Anglers Club: control 35 miles of water from Ashton Basin in Preston, to near Morecambe (www.pikeanglersclub.co.uk/lancaster-canal)

Angling clubs/Tackle shops/Permits:
Kendal DAC (www.kdac.webeden.co.uk) Tickets from Morecambe Angling Centre LA4 5PB (01524 832332)
The PAC (www.pikeanglersclub.co.uk) also control a great deal of fishing.

Trivia

The Lancaster Kendal Canal is one of just a few 'contour canals' – meaning waterways that follow the landscape on an even plane with no locks built.

Leeds & Liverpool Canal

*

Main species: Roach, bream, tench, perch, pike, carp

Notable catches: Pike 25.00, Perch 2.08

This beast of a canal runs some 127 miles, connecting (yes, you guessed it) Leeds and Liverpool. There is a massive amount of water here, with huge potential for anyone who doesn't mind a walk. A few starting points are noted below, but this is a phenomenal waterway for the pioneering angler.

Northern towpath warrior Steve Sutton sums it up perfectly: 'When I was growing up everyone in the North West used to slag the fishing off saying there were no decent fish on the canal. I disagreed and absolutely loved proving everyone wrong!' The fish here can take a fair bit of legwork to track down, but the results can be epic. Steve's efforts alone have banked specimen perch, weighty carp and pike to a mighty 25lbs. Nor is it all about the net busters – roach fishing here can be top class.

With stocks of silver fish high, it's inevitable that specimen pike follow, like this beast from the Leeds & Liverpool Canal. And I don't mean Steve Sutton.

Seriously under-rated fishing – as Steve Sutton proves with another canal specimen.

Trivia

On the Leeds and Liverpool at Bootle in 2013, teenager Kelly Cooney heroically saved the lives of a baby and childminder, after a gust of wind had carried the push-chair of 18-month old Amelia Yates into the canal, taking the pair with it.

Recommended locations: Try Bingley (Dowley Gap Swing Bridge to Swine Lane Bridge) for roach and skimmers on pinkie and ground bait in summer, bread punch in winter. Gorst Lane at Burscough for similar plus big bream to worm.

Maghull, Merseyside (Liverpool DAA): A good bet for skimmers, perch and bonus tench to worm and caster baits.
Newley Marina: Well worth a try for carp and pike.
Burscough, Heaton Bridge and Scarisbrick (Wigan DAA): All productive areas for roach.
Botany Bay, Chorley (Wigan DAA): A productive area for skimmers, especially pegs by the motorway bridge.
Rufford Arm (Wigan DAA): This branch of the Leeds-Liverpool Canal has a good head of silverfish, but is also known for healthy stocks of eels, some cracking tench and the occasional large carp.

Angling clubs/Tackle shops/Permits: Bingley AC, Wigan DAA (wigandaa.org.uk), Johnsons Angling Centre (01515 255574), Burscough Angling (01704 896252)

Historic and beautiful: the Leeds & Liverpool at Saltaire.

You'll find a wide range of species as well as a rich history on the Leeds & Liverpool Canal.

Liverpool DAA (liverpooldaa.com), tickets from Johnsons or Croxteth Angling Centre (L11 9AZ)
Don't miss: The beautiful and historic small town of Saltaire is a majestic reminder of northern England's industrial past, featuring eateries, shops and a special visitors centre (and the fishing's not bad either). More info at: www.saltairevillage.info

Macclesfield Canal

Main species: Roach, perch, ruffe, eels, carp

Something of a late project, with railways already a threat, the Macclesfield Canal was nevertheless completed in 1831. It is a pretty waterway, although quite heavily coloured due to its connection to the Trent and Mersey at Hall Green. Tends to fish best in the autumn and early spring when boat traffic is reduced.

Recommended areas: Astbury, near A34 Congleton Road (Warrington AA): A feature-filled and productive stretch, with odd ghost carp as well as traditional species. Try groundbait and maggot or worm.
Angling clubs/Tackle shops & Permits: Warrington Anglers AA (www.warrington-anglers.org.uk) Season tickets only, from local tackle shops.
Lymm AC (www.lymmanglersclub.com)
Don't miss: The canal has a series of pretty 'roving bridges' (or 'Snake Bridges' to locals), designed to let horses towing barges switch sides where the towpath changes banks.

Manchester Ship Canal

Main species: Roach, perch, bream, chub, pike, carp
Notable catches: Bream 7.08, Carp 30.00

This grand, relatively modern northern waterway has had something of a grubby history. It's reputation as a dirty water was not all local gossip either. Waste water and drains once tipped directly into the canal. My Dad, who grew up in Manchester, still recalls the unfortunately placed notices on city buses, warning passengers 'DO NOT SPIT ON THIS BUS' immediately followed with 'USE THE MANCHESTER SHIP CANAL.'

The better news is that things are cleaning up: quite literally, to the tune of a £90 million plan, involving entire new sewers. The fish population is sure to benefit. Not that the current state of the canal is barren. With a steady tow and depths from 13ft to an incredible 60ft in places, visiting anglers tend to favour feeder or legering tactics for all but fishing right at the edge. Sometimes feeders of 2oz or heavier are required just to hold still.

This is one of the largest and most imposing canals you could ever encounter, with some steep banks and limited access areas besides the sheer scale of the thing.

..........Trivia..........

L.S. Lowry's painting of the park, 'Good Friday, Daisy Nook' (1946) sold for a staggering £3,772,000 – a record for his work.

Trivia

Salford Friendly Anglers' Society is the world's oldest fishing club, formed in 1817, well before the Manchester Ship Canal was ever dug.

But the spoils are there for the dedicated angler, with rumours of fish that would smash current UK canal records. I would advise great caution however, with the wake created by some of the vast ships that travel the canal, as well as some dicey banks and huge depths of water.

Recommended areas:
Salford Quays (Salford Friendly AS): Some huge fish reside here, if you can find them. Match tactics pick up fine bream and roach, while specimen hunters find some huge carp and the odd large pike. Access is restricted due to ships so please check rules.

Angling clubs/Tackle shops & Permits: Salford Friendly Angling Society (www.salfordfriendlyanglers.co.uk). Also some free fishing with EA licence.
Trafford Angling Supplies, Stretford M32 0AY (0161 864 1211)
Monton Bait and Tackle, Eccles M30 0QN (0161 707 7155)

Don't miss: For canal buffs, the Barton Swing Aqueduct is unique (you can proudly bore your friends by telling them you've seen the world's only swing aqueduct).

New Junction Canal

Main species: Roach, bream, hybrids, chub, perch
Notable catches: Perch 4.00, Chub 5.08

A hefty old canal with widths of 90ft and depths to 10ft make this a dependable year-round venue. Pole tactics work at the bottom of the near shelf, while feeder tactics also work to the far side. Feeding should be done with caution, especially on occasions when a strong tow kicks in!

Recommended areas: Skyehouse Lock and Thorne (Doncaster AA): Both these locations hold plenty of skimmers that respond well to ground bait feeder tactics. Thorne also has decent chub.
Barnaby Dun (Doncaster AA): Good for roach close in, but also worth trying bigger baits for chub and specimen perch.

Angling clubs/Tackle shops & Permits: Doncaster AA (www.ddaa.co.uk), York Tackle YO10 5HD (09104 411210)

Pocklington Canal

Main species: Roach, perch, bream, tench, pike

This broad, sometimes picturesque canal runs between south of Pocklington to the River Derwent. The town end is pegged and offers year-round sport for silver fish, while heading into the countryside it becomes wilder and weedier with good sport for pike and tench.

Recommended areas: Canal Head & East Cottingworth (YDAA): Good mixed catches on pole or waggler tactics, as well as winter pike fishing.

Disabled access: The Pocklington end at 'Canal Head' has level platforms and good access.
Angling clubs/Tackle shops & Permits: York DAA (www.ydaa.org.uk)

Peak Forest Canal

Main species: Roach, perch, gudgeon, carp, pike

A pokey little affair divided into two pounds, there is nevertheless some decent mixed fishing here at low cost. Winter roach fishing can be reasonable on bread, or for the more determined there are also a few carp present.

Recommended areas: Try around Stockport itself for roach, with pinkies or bread punch.

Angling clubs/Tackle shops & Permits: Stockport and District AA, tickets and info from Hazel Grove Angling Centre, Stockport SK7 6DG (01625 858643)

Ripon Canal

Main species: Roach, bream, carp
This dainty canal was restored in the 1990s and now contains some good fish stocks, not least of all carp that run to over 20lbs to stalking style tactics.
Recommended areas: Try Ripon, with boilies for carp, bread for silver fish.
Angling clubs/Tackle shops/Permits: Harrogate Angling Supplies HG2 7LG (01423 883270)

Rochdale Canal

Main species: Roach, perch, bream, tench, pike
Notable catches: Tench 5.00

A classic, narrow Cut with a good mix of species, the Rochdale can produce some decent roach fishing, but perhaps the real highlight are the tench.

Recommended locations:
Boarshaw Cemetery/Boarshaw Road Bridge (Heywood DAA): A good bet for skimmers and also tench on pole or waggler.
Firwood Park, Oldham (Waterway Wanderers): Good silver fish nets, but also the chance of tench. Try the far shelf or down the track with worm and caster.

Angling clubs/Tackle shops & Permits: Oldham Angling (01616 241973) Heywood DAA (www. heywoodanddistrictblogspot.co.uk)

Rufford Canal

See Leeds-Liverpool Canal

Sankey Canal

Main Species: Roach, bream, ide, crucians, carp, perch, eels

Cutting its way from St Helens to Widnes, the Sankey Canal (aka the Sankey Brook Navigation or St Helens Canal) adds a dash of local colour in more ways than one. As well as traditional species, some sections contain interesting mixed stocks supplemented by local angling clubs.

Recommended locations:
Spike Island (Warrington AA): Bream

feature in this section and towards Carterhouse, while the canal basin itself is reputed to contain carp to 30lbs, plus the occasional (confused) flounder from the Mersey!

Upper & Lower Pound, Newton-le-Willows, Merseyside (Newton-le-Willows AA): Interesting mixed catches possible with captive stocks. This is the place to catch crucians or even a canal ide!

Angling clubs/Tackle shops & Permits: Warrington AA (www.warrington-anglers.org.uk), Newton-le-Willows AC (www.newtonanglers.co.uk) Widnes Angling Centre WA8 7RJ (01514 200940),

Don't miss: For canal anoraks, the Sankey Viaduct is an impressive slice of engineering from Industrial Revolution England.

Selby Canal

Main species: Roach, perch, bream, tench

This 6 mile canal connects to the River Ouse and has mixed fishing right through the town of Selby. It has most of the usual suspects, but some particularly fine perch and tench.

Recommended areas: Selby (York DAA): Chopped worm and caster recommended here for tench and large perch. Also a good head of pike for winter sport.

Angling clubs/Tackle shops & Permits: York DAA (www.ydaa.org.uk), tickets from Mitre Angling Centre (01904 654841)

Shropshire Union Canal (Northern Section)

Main species: Roach, perch, bream, eels, gudgeon, chub

The 'Shroppie' is a lengthy beast, not to mention a confusing one. We deal in this book with connected waterways such as the Llangollen Canal separately, but the northernmost waters of this grand waterway are also well worth looking into for some fine mixed fishing and season tickets at silly prices, typically well below £20.

Recommended areas:

Chester Zoo (Waterway Wanderers): Excellent value fishing behind the zoo, with plenty of skimmers. Try caster for the best stamp of fish.

Nantwich, Cheshire (Nantwich AS): Roach, perch, gudgeon and bream make up excellent mixed nets. Pinkie and groundbait works for plenty of bites.

Henhull Wides (Wybunbury AA): A short but popular section, prolific for mixed catches on pole or feeder.

Lower Basin, Ellesmere Port: Bream, perch and eels, as well as odd pike here.

Angling clubs/Tackle shops/Permits:

Nantwich AS (www.nantwichangling.co.uk)

Wybunbury AA (www.wybunanglers.btck.co.uk)

Lymm AC (www.lymmanglersclub.com)

Stainforth & Keadby Canal

Main species: Roach, bream, hybrids, perch, rudd, eels, tench, carp

Notable catches: Tench 8.00

A bigger, deeper affair than your typical narrow boat canal, this waterway has typical depths of 9ft plus as well as wide sections that make feeder tactics handy as well as an inside pole line. A host venue for major national matches in the past, there is an excellent mix of both bread and butter species (the roach fishing can be phenomenal) as well as bonus tench and occasional big carp and pike.

Recommended locations: The canal basin in Keadby (Scunthorpe AA) has good depth and is 120 yards wide. Numerous bream and skimmers fall to feeder tactics here – try dead red maggots or worm on the hook.
Godnow Bridge (Scunthorpe AA): A consistent area with roach, rudd and perch featuring, as well as bonus tench and bream.
Thorne (Thorne DAA): Excellent roach fishing even through winter frosts, also skimmers, perch and resident pike.

Angling clubs/Tackle shops & Permits: Scunthorpe AA (scunthorpeangling.co.uk), Thorne DAA (tickets on bank). Permits from Scunthorpe Angling Centre (01724 849815), Chapmans Angling (DN16 2HF), or Stainforth Angling Centre (01302 846623)

Sheffield & Tinsley Canal
*

Main species: Roach, hybrids, bream, perch, pike, carp
Notable catches: Carp 31.08

Industrial-looking it might be but this waterway, running through the heart of the Steel City, is one of the most underrated coarse fisheries of the north. For dedicated specialist anglers, there are some cracking carp and pike to be caught. It's

The Stainforth & Keadby boasts some classic old-school roach fishing.

A quick cast in the Steel City: populations of roach and hybrids are staggeringly high at present, with huge catches possible in Sheffield.

the roach fishing that is truly eye-opening however, with nets to over 20lbs possible on maggot, caster or hemp seed.

Recommended locations:
City Centre, Sheffield: The marina is a no-fishing zone, but try access from Wharf St/South Quay Drive and walk away from the canal basin for fantastic mixed fishing, with plenty of roach and hybrids.
Tinsley (free fishing): Try near the Meadowhall Centre for some phenomenal roach fishing. Hemp or caster pick out samples over 1lb, while the area also offers decent winter pike sport.
Angling clubs/Tackle shops/Permits: Tinsley DAC (01709 830535), also plenty of free fishing. Local tackle shops are your best starting point for ticket info, and in this respect you're spoilt for choice: Billy Clarke Tackle S2 4UB (www.billyclarke.co.uk), Ian's Fishing Tackle S2 1FH (www.iansfishingtackle.co.uk), Kerfoot's Fishing Tackle S5 8GW, Fishing Republic S9 3QD (www.fishingrepublic.co.uk)

Don't miss: The charmingly-named *Noose & Gibbet Inn* is a good place for a pint and is also a stone's throw from the spot where the last man in England was hanged, before being put on display at the Inn site!

Trivia

One of the last canals in commerical use, the Trent and Mersey was still used for shifting cargo well into the 1960s.

South Yorkshire Navigation Canal (aka River Don Navigation)

Main species: Roach, perch, bream, chub

A big and sometimes gritty beast of a channel, the Don Navigation is both a challenge and a treat rolled into one. It might not always look it, but there are good mixed stocks in residence. Feeder or pole fishing are well worth a try, but specialists will also find action with pike.

Recommended areas: Kilnhurst (Kilnhurst DAA): Mixed bags of roach and perch, try groundbait with squats or pinkies.

Angling clubs/Tackle shops & Permits: Kilnhurst DAA – Tickets from Paul's Fishing Tackle DN12 4HU (01709 862558)

Trent & Mersey Canal

Main species: Roach, perch, bream, chub, pike
Notable catches: Roach 2.01, Bream 8.03, Chub 5.00

The northern end of the Trent and Mersey canal continues with many miles of quality mixed fishing. Some species, such as zander, tend to thin out but as well as roach and traditional favourites you'll also find carp in certain locations.

Recommended areas:
Northwich to Middlewich, Cheshire (Nantwich AC): Plenty of roach to float tactics and maggot and caster baits.

Angling clubs/Tackle shops & Permits: Much of the water is shared by the South Cheshire Angling Club Consortium, which includes: Nantwich AC (www.nantwichangling.co.uk), South Cheshire AC

Ulverston Canal

Main species: Roach, rudd, perch, tench, bream, eels, carp, pike
Notable catches: Tench 7.00, Eel 4.00

Only a very short canal at just one mile, this Cumbrian venue is nonetheless a remarkable little venue. Said to be the 'deepest, widest and straightest' canal in the UK, its purpose was to provide the town of Ulverston with a port. It has terrific mixed stocks but is particularly well regarded as a tench water. Nets of over 50lb are possible in the summer, with individual fish often in the 4-6lb class, so don't tackle up too light! Pike are also a presence here, with fish running well into double figures.

Recommended locations: See club site for info.
Disabled access: There are 60 flat, solid match style pegs at the sea end of the canal.
Angling clubs: Ulverston AA (www.ulverstonangling.org) Tickets available online.

SCOTLAND

The rugged terrain and sparser population of Scotland go some way to explaining why there are only a handful of canals north of the border. Nevertheless, the few that do exist are unique places, both historically fascinating and distinctly fishy. Populations of trout and carp certainly add interest for both Scots and visitors alike.

Caledonian Canal

Main species: Brown trout, occasional perch and pike

Situated in beautiful surroundings and Ben Nevis in the background, this great waterway is worth a visit for its sheer uniqueness alone, connecting four Lochs (Loch Lochy, Loch Oich, Loch Ness and Loch Dochfour).

You won't find abundant stocks of coarse fish, but it probably has more brown trout than any other Cut in the British Isles! Fishing with a worm as bait is the easiest way to catch one, although spinning and flyfishing will also work. The water is very clear and thus on hot, bright days, expect the fish to lie deep. The trout seem to average about three to the pound, although a quick look in the

Trivia

The Caledonian is Britain's most northerly canal.

margins reveals hordes of sticklebacks and minnows. An early or late session away from the holiday crowds could well be the way to tussle with a big, predatory brown.

Recommended locations: Parking is available just beyond Fort William at Banavie. There are trout all along this waterway. Try a float-fished worm at different depths, or flyfishing if there is cloud cover and breeze.

Angling clubs/Tackle shops & Permits: Free fishing with EA Licence.
Don't miss: Neptune's Staircase is a must-see for any canal enthusiast. With eight consecutive locks, it raises vessels a towering 70 feet above sea level, giving boat crews a headache in the process.

One of the many bonuses of canal fishing in Scotland: a beautiful wild brownie from the Caledonian Canal.

Crinan Canal

Main species: Brown trout

'Britain's most beautiful shortcut' is a nine mile stretch of canal in the Kintyre Peninsula. It contains plenty of brown trout and even has the odd salmon running through its course! With some 9,000 boats using this waterway every year, however, you'd be well advised to make an early start or have a crack at tea time, when the boaters aren't out in force.

Recommended locations: Try between locks 9 and 13 for trout. Float-fished worm is the easiest way, but spinners or flies also work.
Angling clubs: Free fishing with EA Licence

Forth and Clyde Canal *

Main species: Roach, perch, bream, tench, gudgeon, pike, eels, carp
Notable catches: Carp 34.12, Pike 21.00

'No trout in there, mate'. Actually, there are stacks of them.

Forth & Clyde: never a dull moment.

Scotland's main man-made waterway has both urban and quieter, feature-filled sections. At 34 miles long with 39 locks, it is a key part of Glasgow's industrial heritage, once accommodating sea-going vessels transporting goods and raw materials.

These days, leisure use has taken over, and it is one of the most important coarse fisheries north of the border.

Most common canal species are present. Mixed catches of roach, perch and bream are to be had along its length, but stocks of larger coarse fish are also present, including some belting specimens. The tench fishing can be excellent with traditional baits such as worm and corn. Pike are present throughout too, and while most are jacks, there is always the chance of a double. Perhaps the most exciting prospect of all are the carp, however, with past stock fish growing on well. A 20-pounder is a possibility to the dedicated specialist, while the canal also holds the Scottish record carp at over 34 pounds.

Recommended locations: Firhill Basin, Glasgow: A noted spot for tench and carp. These big, wily resident carp can require perseverance, but there are fish well into double figures.

Cadder to Kirkintilloch: Try pole or waggler on this section for decent bags of roach, perch and skimmers. The urban areas stay a little warmer in the winter, providing year-round sport.

Dullatur/Wynford Lock: The waters here are wide, exposed and deep, making this an ideal area to try the feeder for bream, or a spot of pike fishing.

Angling clubs/Tackle shops & Permits: Fishing here requires membership of the SFCA (Scottish Federation of Coarse Anglers). An absolute bargain at £5 a season, or free for youngsters, see www.sfca.co.uk for registration and further details.

Don't miss: The Falkirk Wheel is a unique modern feat of engineering. This rotating boat lift stands at an impressive 35 metres and is a world first! There is also

Trivia

The Forth and Clyde is Scotland's earliest constructed, and longest, canal.

a visitors centre (FK1 4RS) and organised activities for the family (although we think you'd probably rather be fishing!) www.thefalkirkwheel.co.uk

Monkland Canal, Glasgow

*

Main species: Roach, perch, pike, tench, carp

Notable catches: Roach 1.12, Carp 22.00

An unlikely gem if ever there was one, the Monkland Canal is a pretty and prolific stretch of water running right through the suburbs of Glasgow. Once linked to the Forth and Clyde, it now exists in isolated sections, which disappear mysteriously under Glasgow's road network. Despite missing sections, it is very much the story of a waterway saved from the brink. If anything, its non-navigable status is a bonus for anglers. The waters here are clear, weedy in places and very fishy.

Perhaps the most notable target species present are the roach. Big, wily red fins thrive here. I took several fine fish to 1¾lb on a flying visit, but there are roach bigger than this present and a 2-pounder could be a distinct possibility. These creatures are no mugs however, and with a steady tow often on the water, your presentation must be spot-on. Bread flake is the ideal bait, either float fished or even presented on a light legering set-up. Carp are also present for the patient specialist angler, while plenty of jack pike make for good sport on lure or fly tactics in the clear water. Free fishing is also a bonus – although the Monklands is crying out for the stewardship and sensible rules of a decent angling club.

Recommended locations: Try the Drumpellier Country Park area (access via roads off Drumpellier Avenue, and the small bridge off Deanbank Rd) for quality roach, jack pike and odd carp. The end of this section by Blair Road has a streamy inflow which is also good for roach. Further east, the canal springs up once more, and again roach thrive in water that has a fair current for a canal. Don't forget a loaf of white bread!

Angling clubs/Tackle shops & Permits: Free fishing with EA licence

Don't miss: Look for 'Scotland vs Wales, Monkland Canal' on YouTube, which features beautifully dated 1990s footage of this pretty canal prior to a historic fishing contest, complete with brilliantly bonkers technicolour graphics and Casio keyboard soundtrack!

Union Canal

Main species: Roach, perch, bream, tench, pike

Connecting Edinburgh to the Forth and Clyde Canal via the Falkirk Wheel, the Union Canal is another accessible mixed fishery with decent stocks of coarse fish. Formerly in a state of disuse, increased boat traffic has at least saved the Cut from problems with excessive weed and silt – although you still have to find the fish.

Recommended areas: Newbridge and Polmont: Worth a go for roach, perch and other species on the pole, a few pike too.
Broxburgh to Winchburn: Good stretch for roach shoals. Try maggot and groundbait, or bread punch if the water is clear
Linlithgow: Worth a try for pike on bait, or try lures and flies in clear water.
Craiglockhart: The canal is distinctly urban here, but there are pockets of roach and perch, as well as jack pike.

Angling clubs/Tackle shops & Permits:
SFCA (Scottish Federation of Coarse Anglers) control fishing on the Union, see www.sfca.co.uk for registration and further details.

For further info on angling, attractions and other information on Scotland's Canals, another excellent resource is www.scottishcanals.co.uk

NORTHERN IRELAND

Although renowned for its fine rivers and loughs, a less celebrated feature of angling in Northern Ireland is its great canals. Some once busy waterways, such as the Ulster Canal, might have fallen into decay but some affordable, top quality fishing remains on other towpaths. Healthy populations of rudd, roach and pike are perhaps the pick of the typical canal species. Nor should these smaller waters be written off for specimens – individual pike over 30lb have been landed.

Lagan Navigation Canal
(includes Broadwater Canal)

Main species: Roach, perch, bream, hybrids, pike

Near the town of Moira, this canal offers around a mile of peaceful fishing. Much of the old Lagan is derelict, but the Broadwater Canal is one section that still offers good fishing. The usual roach, bream and hybrids feature, but the fishery is also noted as a productive spot for winter pike with a double figure predator very much a possibility.

Recommended areas:
Broadwater Canal, near Aghalee (off B105 Soldierstown Road): Winter pike fishing, as well as plenty of roach on this shallow stretch of the Lagan.
South of Dunmurry: Quiet waters and mixed fishing for the angler who travels light.
Tackle shops: Loughview Angling Centre, Lurgan BT66 6NQ (028 38342777)
Permits: DCAL permit required.

Movanagher Canal

Main species: Roach, perch, bream, hybrids, pike
Notable catches: Pike 30.12

Situated near Kilrea, there is just over half a mile of fishing here with abundant coarse fish stocks, including some cracking pike. An especially handy place to fish when the rivers are in flood.

Recommended areas: Off the B64, near Movanagher Fish Farm (see www.nidirect.gov.uk site):
Disabled access: Three dedicated platforms by the car park
Tickets: DCAL permit required
Tackle shops: Mid Antrim Angling Centre BT43 6AW (028 25648159)

Newry Canal

Main species: Roach, perch, bream, hybrids, pike
Notable catches: Bream 5.08, Pike 15.00

First dug to transport coal and other goods towards Dublin from the north, the Newry Canal was once a busy waterway. Railways might have put paid to that, but large sections of the Newry still exist in a quieter state and the canal is now a protected area, offering some good mixed coarse fishing. Pike feature throughout, whilst roach fishing can offer some classic year round sport – matches have been won with nets to well over 30lb even in the depths of winter. The section starting at Newry is usually the preferred option, as it is a much wider, more open ship-style canal. Other sections are narrower and more neglected, but offer quiet waters to explore.

Recommended areas:
Newry (Loughs Agency): Decent bream and pike possible, as well as roach at this end, which includes Albert Basin, a match stretch noted for year round roach sport. Also expect pike.
Scarva: is just one access point for several miles of canal, worth roving for pike in particular.

.........Trivia.........

Said to pre-date the Bridgewater Canal by 20 years, the Newry is arguably Britain's earliest 'true' canal.

Angling clubs/Tackle shops/Permits: A Loughs Agency permit is required (see www.loughs-agency.org for permit and further fishing details). Bait and supplies nearby at Smyths Angling and Outdoors, Newry BT34 1DQ (028 30252332).

Portna Canal

Main species: Roach, perch, bream, hybrids, pike
Notable fish: Pike 25.00

A short canal, but one with good access and noted for quality pike fishing, especially when the River Bann is in winter flood and fish come here to shelter. A double figure fish is always a possibility. Fishing is restricted to beneath the locks.

Recommended areas: Portna is just off the A54 Kilrea-Portglenone Road (*see* www.nidirect.gov.uk for further info).
Tickets: DCAL Permit

For Information on several of Northern Ireland's canals, see also www.nidirect.gov.uk/angling

DCAL permits can be bought online for several canals, using the following outrageously long link: https://applications.dcal-fishingni.gov.uk/AnglingPermits-Booking/PurchasePermits.aspx

The national canal record bream of 10lb 4oz taken by Tyrone Norah from the Exeter Ship.

Ian Breech's record canal grass carp of 31lb 8oz.

Russ Hilton with his canal record rudd of 2lb 5oz.

Dan Sales' record canal perch of 4lb 4oz.

UK Canal Record Fish List

SPECIES	WEIGHT (lbs/oz/dr)	CANAL	CAPTOR	YEAR
Barbel	16.00	Oxford	Alan Holmes	2009
Bream	10.04	Exeter Ship	Tyrone Norah	2012
Carp	46.04	Grand Union	Bill Phillips	2013
Chub	7.03	Monmouth & Brecon	Matt Jones	2011
Crucian Carp	2.08	Grand Union, Beds	Lawrence Watson	2011
Eel	9.03	Grand Union, Herts	Paul Chapman	1998
Grass Carp	31.08	Gloucester	Ian Breech	2008
Grayling	3.14	Driffield Canal	D Sawyer	1967
Gudgeon	0.01.12	Grand Union	Neil Williams	2010
Orfe	5.02	Grand Union	Unknown	2005
Perch	4.04	Grand Union	Dan Sales	2012
Pike	32.06	Kennet & Avon	Simon Allsop	2010
Roach	2.04	Gloucester	S. Swan	1971
Rudd	2.05	Grand Western	Russell Hilton	2011
Silver Bream	2.01	Grand Union, Warks	Keith Jobling	2011
Trout (rainbow)	6.08	Driffield	James Walsh	2006
Trout (brown)	3.14	Grand Union	Malcolm Nieman	2013
Tench	8.08	Leicester	M. Foode	1950
Zander	18.00	Ashby	Andy Spring	2012

UK Five-Hour Canal Match Record

107 lbs (Carp) Shropshire Union Canal (Autherley), Paul Turner, 2010

USEFUL ORGANISATIONS & SITES

The Canal and River Trust/ Waterway Wanderers Scheme (canalrivertrust.org)
Plenty here on activities, heritage and how you can get involved from the main governing body when it comes to British canals. The site also includes a full list of fishable canal stretches on the Waterway Wanderers scheme – a fantastic value fishing ticket with over 200 miles of water.

The Angling Trust (www.anglingtrust.net)
An organisation every angler should join, working hard to campaign on all current angling issues and threats to freshwater habitats, not least of all canals. Members also get a discount on the Waterway Wanderers ticket.

Environment Agency
Like any freshwater fisheries, canals need the eyes and ears of anglers and the EA is the body to which you should report any immediate concerns. Particular current issues are pollution and fish thefts – but the Agency can only act if we are prepared to make the call. An excellent idea is to store their emergency number on your mobile (currently 0800 807060).

DG Fishing (www.dgfishing.co.uk)
The author's site has free content, beautiful photography and a lively blog that often features canal fishing exploits.

Fly For Coarse
While we've only had space in passing here to describe the method, flyfishing can be excellent for a whole range of species, especially on clearer canals. The author's book *Flyfishing For Coarse Fish* goes into much greater depth, while www.flyforcoarse.com is a dedicated site and special competition for this growing branch of angling.

GUGGS, or the Grand Union Gobio Gobio Society, to give its full title, is a brilliant, fun-loving society dedicated to gudgeon fishing. Their site, complete with specimen records, is guaranteed to make you grin: www.guggs.net

Idler's Quest (idlersquest.blogspot.com)
Of all the blogs that regularly tour the nation's canals, Jeff Hatt's is one of the very finest. Expect wit and wisdom, direct from the towpath.

INDEX

Other coarse fishing titles from Merlin Unwin Books

Flyfishing for Coarse Fish
Pocket Guide to Fishing Knots
The Secret Carp
Falling in Again
Fishing with Emma
The Fisherman's Bedside Book
Confessions of a Carp Fisher
Fishing with Harry

www.merlinunwin.co.uk